Secular Days,
Sacred Moments

Secular Days, Sacred Moments

The *America* Columns of Robert Coles

Robert Coles

Edited by David D. Cooper

MICHIGAN STATE UNIVERSITY PRESS · EAST LANSING

Copyright © 2013 by Robert Coles; Foreword © 2013 by Michigan State University

 Publication of this book was supported by an award from the MSU Foundation.

These columns were originally published in *America*. They are reprinted with the permission of Robert Coles and America Press, Inc., 106 West 56th Street, New York, NY 10019.

♾ The paper used in this publication meets the minimum requirements of ANSI/NISO Z39.48-1992 (R 1997) (Permanence of Paper).

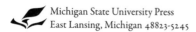 Michigan State University Press
East Lansing, Michigan 48823-5245

Printed and bound in the United States of America.

19 18 17 16 15 14 13   1 2 3 4 5 6 7 8 9 10

LIBRARY OF CONGRESS CATALOGING-IN-PUBLICATION DATA
Coles, Robert.
[Essays. Selections]
Secular days, sacred moments : the America columns of Robert Coles / by Robert Coles ; edited by David D. Cooper.
pages cm
Essays by Robert Coles herein first appeared as columns in the America National Catholic Weekly.
ISBN 978-1-61186-073-3 (pbk. : alk. paper) — ISBN 978-1-60917-358-6 (ebook)
1. United States—Religion—History—20th century. 2. Religion and sociology—United States—History—20th century. 3. United States—Social conditions—20th century. 4. Christianity—20th century. I. Cooper, David D. II. America. Contained in (work): III. Title.
BL2525.C628 2013
277.3'082—dc23
2012028151

Book design by Sharp Des!gns, Lansing, Michigan
Cover design by Erin Kirk New
Cover photograph is used courtesy of the photographer, David Cooper. All rights reserved.

green press INITIATIVE Michigan State University Press is a member of the Green Press Initiative and is committed to developing and encouraging ecologically responsible publishing practices. For more information about the Green Press Initiative and the use of recycled paper in book publishing, please visit *www.greenpressinitiative.org*.

Visit Michigan State University Press at *www.msupress.org*

Contents

Foreword

The thirty-one short essays by Robert Coles gathered together here appeared as columns in the Catholic weekly *America*. The first was published in November 1996 under the banner "Secular Days, Sacred Moments"—a title Coles attributes to his friend and mentor, Dorothy Day. In that inaugural column Coles recalls a conversation he had with Day forty years earlier when he admitted his uneasy feelings and fears as a medical student working part-time at Day's Catholic Worker soup kitchen in New York City. It was one thing, he pointed out to her, to encounter those in need in a medical clinic or a hospital under the established (and safe) rules of medical authority—quite another thing to serve the poor in a soup line and face "their unpredictability, their enormous vulnerability, their not rare outbursts." Day could empathize with Coles's predicament. "A hospital offers the best of the secular world," she reminded him. "Here [at the soup kitchen] we are trying hard to do the work of faith."

This defining episode scribes for Coles, in effect, a narrative arc that he hopes to follow in his upcoming "Secular Days, Sacred Moments" columns. Our vulnerability and humility, our willingness to summon candid self-criticism, our courage to let down the shields of position and authority . . . these acts of contrition, Coles implies, serve as gateways to "encounters with the sacred." Subsequent installments at that narrative and existential threshold came regularly in *America*, roughly once a month, until February 2000.

While not "religious" in the conventional sense, Robert Coles has always been drawn to the social witness of religious lives. It is an attraction he traces to his parents. They often discussed religious and spiritual matters with Coles and his brother at the dinner table or during long walks when the boys were growing up in Boston. Later, during medical school at Columbia University's College of Physicians and Surgeons, Coles would often slip off to Catholic churches where he could be left alone, "left to pray or sit and day-dream." He read the Bible and joined other medical students in a New Testament study group, often taking on the role of devil's advocate. While still in medical school in the early 1950s, Coles fell under the bracing influence of contemporary theologians Reinhold Niebuhr and Paul Tillich, whose courses he audited at Union Theological Seminary and, later, the University of Chicago during a psychiatry residency. Coles was especially interested in their mixture of religious insight and political sensibility, and the way their systematic theologies made plenty of room for hopefulness *and* skepticism—later hallmarks, it turns out, of Coles's monthly *America* columns. Throughout his career, he drew much inspiration, as well, from modern religious figures such as Dietrich Bonhoeffer, Dorothy Day, and Simone Weil, all of whom Coles wrote about extensively. His teaching—in particular, "Literature of Social Reflection," the famous Harvard College course Coles offered for so many years—tapped deeply into the religious wellsprings of novelists Walker Percy, Flannery O'Connor, Georges Bernanos, and others. Probably no writer or public intellectual of our era has been as sensitive to the role of faith in the lives of ordinary Americans, especially the poor and the distressed Coles came to know during his extensive documentary fieldwork, those for whom religious faith, he once remarked in an interview, "is a means of voicing all kinds of revolutionary passions." Coles's *The Spiritual Life of Children* (1990) earned him further credibility in the national conversation over faith, spirituality, and public life; the book even broke onto the *New York Times* Best Seller List, a distinction that none of Coles's earlier *Children of Crisis* books achieved. While cultivating a lifelong suspicion of ideologies and easy fixes to the dilemmas and the challenges of the modern condition, Robert Coles nonetheless readily admits that the "back-and-forthness between faith and doubt is the story of my life."

So Coles was particularly well positioned in 1996 to continue telling that story in the pages of *America* at the intersection of "Secular Days, Sacred Moments." Coles understood that crossroads as a meeting ground for the Catholic commitment to faith, the church's respect for reason, and the value Coles himself placed on personal responsibility and self-insight honed by years of psychiatric practice. It is a place where he could struggle with moral questions as they surface in the concrete particulars of everyday life: such as, "what the devil does this life mean," as he put it in the introduction to *Harvard Diary I* (1989), "and how the devil ought we try to live it?" Coles used the *America* columns to engage such questions along a range of subjects constantly refreshed by the sacred/secular dynamic and his personal tug-of-war between faith and doubt, including writers and painters (Thomas Merton, Tillie Olsen, Winslow Homer), his recent reading and film viewing (*Othello, The Thin Red Line*), contemporary events and lingering controversies (busing, homosexuality, the brutality of the Third Reich), recollections of past and present mentors (Erik Erikson; William Carlos Williams; Coles's wife, Jane Hallowell Coles), events of his own daily life (fixing a flat tire along the busy Cambridge Turnpike, recovering from a bike accident), and ordinary encounters with students, patients, neighbors, and friends.

Although Coles had contributed sporadically and sparsely to *America* since 1972, the offer by then-editor Fr. George W. Hunt in September 1996 to submit a regular column on any topic of Coles's choosing came as something of a surprise. As it turned out, Fr. Hunt's timing was perfect. Coles had been writing a regular column on religion and secularity called "Harvard Diary" for the progressive monthly *New Oxford Review* (*NOR*) since 1981. Like *America*, *NOR* was devoted to serious discussion of religion—Catholic, but with an ecumenical bent—and the resonance of religious perspectives with contemporary political, social, cultural, and economic concerns. Similar to his later arrangement with *America*, *NOR* editor Dale Vree started off giving Coles free rein in his choices for column topics. Coles responded by refining his talent for the occasional personal essay in over 150 pieces he contributed during his long tenure as a *NOR* monthly columnist and contributing editor.

As *NOR*'s theological perspectives became more conservative and, eventually, rigid, it became difficult for a non-Catholic like Coles to avoid entanglements over church doctrine. In the summer of 1996 Vree objected to columns Coles submitted that touched on birth control and abortion. "I will spare both of us," Coles quickly responded to Vree, "an extended presentation of my views with respect to the evolution of the *New Oxford Review* and my position as a writer for it." Thanking him for a "long, informal relationship," Coles resigned, effectively immediately. The parting was bittersweet but amicable.

Coming less than a month after the *NOR* separation, the offer from Fr. Hunt at *America* seemed serendipitous, and Coles readily accepted. It should be noted that Fr. Hunt was completely unaware of developments at *NOR*. And Coles himself, characteristically, did not seek out an arrangement with *America*. Nor was there any indication that Coles was gun-shy of writing another personal column for a Catholic periodical. Like *NOR, America* was liberal on social issues, but considerably less prickly on matters concerning theology and moral teaching. Neither scholarly nor catechetical, *America* was a well-respected journal of Catholic opinion widely read by Catholics and non-Catholics alike. It served readers interested in intelligent examination of church and world affairs seen through the lens of Catholic faith and with the eyes of Catholic reason. An editorial commitment to civility, fair-mindedness, diversity of perspective, and high-quality, accessible writing has sustained *America* for nearly a century. During the four years Robert Coles wrote the "Secular Days, Sacred Lives" column, he never locked horns with an editor over Catholic doctrine. In fact, Thomas J. Reese, S.J., who took over as editor in 1998, prodded Coles to take on controversial, hair-trigger issues like homosexuality and the Clinton-Lewinsky affair. Coles gladly obliged.

Taken together, the *NOR* and *America* assignments positioned Robert Coles as a preeminent, durable, and trusted voice in the national conversation over religion and civic life for two decades. Even though it was a time of growing conservatism, crisis among Catholics, and gradual retrenchment of religious orthodoxies, the dividing line between secular life and religious commitment and practice was by no means either faint or fixed during the period. Many thoughtful Americans turned to magazines like *NOR* and *America* as they struggled with moral questions and sought out new ways to configure the connections between religion, spirituality, the social condition of the country, and the felt sphere of their everyday lives.

The value—perhaps the genius—of Robert Coles's regular dispatches on the sacred and the secular is that they took on moral questions openly and honestly. And they did so without Coles tapping into his academic status and prestige or parlaying his considerable reputation as a famous child psychiatrist, public intellectual, and prolific author. In fact, he purposely cultivated an intimate narrative persona as a diarist or a letter writer. Coles often used his monthly columns to probe and question, as he put it, "the assumptions which have informed my work—the values and ideals (and blind spots, too) I've carried around as I've done my teaching, seen my patients." This rare combination of rectitude and authorial modesty gradually earned Coles credibility in the eyes of his readers, and it no doubt contributed to Fr. Hunt's enthusiastic invitation to join the *America* family of writers shortly after Coles removed his name from the *NOR* masthead.

Secular Days, Sacred Moments: The America *Columns of Robert Coles* rounds out a series of Coles's short commentaries on the country's moral temperature during the closing decades of the twentieth century. Two related volumes, edited by Crossroad's publisher Michael Leach, gathered together 111 of Coles's *NOR* columns. The first of these was published by Crossroads in 1989 as *Harvard Diary I: Reflections on the Sacred and the Secular*, the second, in 1997, as *Harvard Diary II: Essays on the Sacred and the Secular.*

I worked closely with Dr. Coles on compiling this latest volume and preparing it for publication. During visits at his home in Concord, Massachusetts, Dr. Coles and I often revisited the topics, the issues, and the particular contexts and circumstances of the *America* commentaries. I was often struck with their continuing vitality and relevance to the first decade of a new century. My goal in editing this collection has been to capitalize upon that freshness while preserving the original context of a serial publication. For example, the columns originally appeared in the *America* masthead under the generic title "Secular Days, Sacred Moments," but the columns themselves did not carry specific titles in each issue's layout. The columns appear here, then, in chronological order with their dates of original publication. I have decided, except in the cases of the last three commentaries, to use each column's original page layout pull quote as a title instead of refitting new, truncated titles. In October 1999, *America* changed its editorial format and started using individual titles. For consistency in the present edition, I selected new pull quotes for the final three columns (October 9, 1999; December 4, 1999; and February 19, 2000).

In preparing this edition, I have used resources held in Michigan State University's extensive archive of Robert Coles's literary and personal papers. In 2007 Dr. Coles donated his papers to Michigan State University's Special Collections for student, general public, and scholarly access and use. The collection—the Robert Coles Papers, MSS 323—spans hundreds of thousands of pages of personal and institutional correspondence, manuscripts and drafts, teaching materials, awards and marginalia, and interviews with Coles from the 1960s to the present. In addition, a separately indexed collection—the *DoubleTake* Archive, MSS 305—contains seventy-eight boxes of valuable archival material from 1995 to 2003 when Coles was editor of *DoubleTake* magazine. In the case of the *America* columns, I was able to check and verify the definitive text of each column by comparing the published version to the original holographic manuscript, the typescript, and the corrected page proofs. I also examined the correspondence between Coles and *America* editors George Hunt and Thomas J. Reese, *NOR* editor Dale Vree, Crossroads editor Michael Leach, and, in some cases, those individuals Coles engages in conversation throughout the columns (Dorothy Day, Erik Erikson, Walker Percy, and some of Coles's former students, for example). Sometimes I consulted the collection to learn more about Coles's position on a topic that surfaces in more than one column (for example, the bruising South Boston busing controversy Coles became embroiled in during the 1970s, or his counseling of terminally ill patients). This important historical, biographical, and legacy resource, along with frequent trips to Concord and numerous telephone conversations with Dr. Coles, made the task of editing this book much more than an academic exercise. It turned into an enterprise of living scholarship. And more than that: the good work of friendship.

DAVID D. COOPER
Paso Robles, California

Secular Days,
Sacred Moments

We're hoping for a few extra moments of the sacred during these long secular days.

I first heard the words I am using as the title for this column from the lips of Dorothy Day—and therein a story. In the middle-1950s I was a medical student in New York City, at Columbia's College of Physicians and Surgeons. In my spare time I worked in a Catholic Worker soup kitchen, and so doing, often felt confused, torn by various and conflicting feelings—a desire to be of help to needy others, but also a fear of them (their unpredictability, their enormous vulnerability, their not rare outbursts). It was one thing to work with poor, hurt, even unsettled or unstable people in a clinic or hospital, under the protection of medical authority, with all its established procedures and rules; it was quite something else to be "out there" on a serving line, handing food to people, trying to make conversation with them.

Years later I pointed out the difference to Dorothy Day, asked her why such an evident disparity in my attitude or feelings. She smiled faintly—a prelude, I knew, to one or another of her sharply knowing observations—and then this: "At the medical center you were working in an imposing setting, and the people who came there knew it. If they 'misbehaved,' they'd have to leave and a policeman would have helped

3

them [do so], if they were reluctant! Here we're trying to offer a 'home' to people for an hour or two (or more): some food, some clothes, some attention and concern. They're not 'on guard,' as they were when they came to see you doctors."

She paused, but only to catch her breath, gather her strength for an elaboration that obviously meant a lot to her, I realized, because she spoke with considerable intensity and quite personally: "I'm not sure you'll agree with what I'm going to say—I'm not even sure I'm right; but I wonder whether the difference isn't spiritual in nature. I mean, a hospital offers the best of the secular world—at least when the doctors are doing a good job. Here we are trying hard to do the work of faith, of love, and I mean we are addressing ourselves, our condition, as well as [that of] these people we've just given some soup and coffee. I know there are similarities—that a truly good doctor wants to offer his or her heart to a patient, as well as put knowledge into action. But I do think that people make distinctions and act accordingly. You go to the hospital and try to be on your best behavior; you come here, and if you're in despair, it's all right to cry out, because the people who run the place, they're also crying out at times, just as Jesus did!"

Again a pause, and then an effort to conclude a further line of reasoning: "I think—I hope—all of us have our secular days, but we're lucky if we can find our sacred moments. I think a doctor treating a patient capably and with respect can be a witness to the sacred, right there in the midst of the secular world. I hope and pray we have our times of witness here, witness to the sacred. You can say that here we're dedicating ourselves to the pursuit of that—the sacred—though with no guarantee that we'll succeed. I guess it always comes down to the same tension—those sacred moments allowed us in our secular days. Maybe we're just a little more ambitious in this place—ambitious spiritually: a dangerous kind of aspiration, because pride can certainly fall upon us, get in our way. But we keep trying. We're hoping for a few extra moments of the sacred during these long secular days, whereas the doctors up there [in the medical center] have other matters on their minds, I'm sure."

This was a not untypical kind of a conversational journey with her, I had by then come to know—an effort to make a spiritual distinction or clarification that was at least partially and ironically thwarted by a surge of humility, a willingness to be candidly self-critical, even to the point of summoning a skepticism of her own conceptual thinking. She was "stumbling," she went on to say, but she was willing to uphold, with whatever necessary qualifications, her sense that most of the time we live our all too (morally, psychologically, spiritually) finite (secular) lives, whereas on occasion (by intent or through luck or as a consequence of our character as it unself-consciously engages with events that come our way) we are graced with the sacred.

I knew better than to ask her to spell out the meaning of "sacred"—I'd once done so, only to see her head lowered. Eventually her silence was followed by an unforgettable comment: "I'm afraid it's the Lord who decides that [what constitutes the sacred.]" She was, by implication, letting me know, yet again, that vanity (here, in the form of intellectual insistence) can be an obstacle to the sacred.

So this life goes, Dorothy Day was indicating: its extended secular time, with all the attendant tasks, responsibilities, commitments, interrupted occasionally by a sacred spell—for the arrival of which we can only pray. It was her hope that in those Catholic Worker communities some of her fellow pilgrims would be lucky enough to be graced by a few encounters with the sacred. But she dared not go further, think of the sacred as something we here can arrange for ourselves, declare ourselves to possess, institutionalize—hence her temporal imagery, itself a kind of contrition. We rise to, seize the secular days, even as we may yearn for those sacred moments that soulwise guide us, define us.

"The doctors, they be strutters. They need teaching."

A few years ago I worked as a volunteer fifth-grade teacher in an elementary school located in an impoverished Boston neighborhood. The children knew I also taught college students, medical students—indeed, this school wasn't all that far from the medical school building where my class met weekly, as a ten-year-old girl reminded me one day. She had been with her mother to see a doctor "over there," a first visit on her part to a hospital, and she had learned a lot: "I never thought there could be all these sick folks in one place!" I told her I'd once been a young doctor there, at the Children's Hospital; I well remembered how crowded the clinics could get. But she suddenly changed tack, told me (and of course, her listening classmates) that she didn't mind "all the people," only "some of them." A pause, as I wondered whether to pursue the matter with the obvious question aimed at finding out which people had met with her disapproval and why—and then, suddenly, this spoken statement: "The doctors, they be strutters. They need teaching."

I took immediate note of the vernacular she had used—these were all Afro-American children save three, whose parents were born in Puerto Rico. I wondered, yet again, whether to make further inquiry of this girl, Cynthia, or hurry back to our spelling lesson, which I'd been trying to accomplish in the face of a certain skepticism on the part of the children not unlike that of William James, George Bernard Shaw, Flannery O'Connor, to name a few writers who have mocked the way we render, letter-wise, certain words. Indeed, this very girl who had just told us of hospital strutters had once written this as a footnote to her spelling test (in which she'd answered all the questions correctly): "Why isn't enuf good enough?" A clever, but sassy one, I'd thought—and I'd resisted the temptation to write "cool!" beside her question. She and others in the room had, of course, heard me many times give the standard justifications for the conventional—we had to live in the world, come to obliging terms with its rules, its authority.

Anyway, I hesitated a bit too long, because a boy sitting across the aisle from Cynthia, Tom by name, asked for details in this briefly insistent way: "Explain yourself." I could have broken in, broken up this stray line of inquiry, this distraction from duty, but I was myself curious—I wondered what had happened to prompt such a wholesale categorization. In no time we were all hearing Cynthia's take on the doctors she'd observed, the doctor who had attended her: "They're busy, they are—and they let you know it. We already can figure it out, that they've got a lot to do, but they want to make sure we don't forget it!" She stopped, and Tom seemed puzzled. He quickly let her know why: "If you're working hard, and you say so—why is that being a strutter?" Cynthia's face registered surprise, impatience, irritation, and she was quick to reply: "They didn't give us credit for understanding anything. They're big on talking, on telling you this and that and something here and there, but they don't listen like they should. You go off on your own, and they'll cut you off."

Yet the boy, Tom, didn't seem convinced. He took the doctors' side: "Give them a break—they're in a rush; they've got to get their job done.

8 ⌣

You can't be polite all the time!" Nods of approval across the room. Cynthia seemed temporarily silenced, even somewhat persuaded: "For sure, it's a lot they have to do. But if you watch them, you'll see them being nice and relaxed with each other, and if it's one of them who comes and interrupts, they'll lend an ear, but if we try to tell them something, they hurry on. My momma's momma was with us, and she's worked for them [white, professional families] for all her life, and she whispered to me that 'the white coats, they've done gone to their heads.'"

She stopped. The tide had turned in her favor—a nearly audible stillness in the room. I was the only one making noise—fidgeting as I contemplated what to do. I sat there visualizing those white coats I once wore; I remembered making sure that my stethoscope was ever so visible over the rim of a pocket. I remembered, too, hurrying some people along, brushing past their remarks in my busy mind—but in an instant, being ready to smile for, carefully pay heed to a fellow physician or, yes, a patient who was of a particular background, who was like me or like what I've learned to want to be.

I shuddered with embarrassment, tried to hide my memories from shaping my facial expression, not to mention my words. I quietly, rather too quietly, suggested that we move on, get back to our spelling. But Cynthia, good teacher that she was, wanted to conclude her lesson decisively, lest we fail to get her intended point. She brought us back to her initial observation: "If they'd listen, they'd learn more; that's how you learn—through your ears, not your mouth." Again, a noticeable silence (a moment of grace, actually); and then a wave of smiles prompted, I decided, by a child's vivid anatomical language that struck a home run in the minds of many of these youngsters—even as I, at last, realized what I needed to do: figure out how to listen better, more.

*Merton and Milosz find common ground in their
skepticism—the distance they put between themselves
and faddish trends.*

For ten years (1958–68) the poet and essayist Czeslaw Milosz and
the poet and monk Thomas Merton wrote letters to one another—many of them searchingly introspective, a few stirringly
confessional. They only met twice, each time briefly. Perhaps the very
distance between them, and a lack of personal acquaintance, made possible
such a candid willingness on the part of both men to share with one
another thoughts they would otherwise (with friends and even family,
one suspects) have kept to themselves. Milosz, for instance, repeatedly
refers to his "self-love," his "wounds of ambition," his tenacious egoism
("imprisoned as I am in my 'I'"). He even wonders whether he might have
been "lying" with respect to what he told a priest in confession. Merton
is no less willing to arraign himself; he terms himself a "bourgeois," "a
prisoner of my class," and wonders whether his religious life isn't a mere
"reaction" against such an inherited position of privilege. He echoes his
correspondent's reservations with respect to the moral and psychological
nature of confession: "But how can one confess to an institution? And
what kind of forgiveness is dispensed by an organization?" Like Milosz,

who abhorred Stalinism yet railed against the French bourgeoisie—trenchant scorn worthy of the Marxist polemical tradition—Merton was ready to criticize power and privilege, even in his own backyard: "Aggressive Catholicism, sure of itself, deeply involved in a power struggle, content to be anti-Communist, gentle to everyone but those who need it, and harsh on them."

To read these letters, to be published this month by Farrar, Straus and Giroux, is to realize how hard it was for many of this century's most energetic moral figures to place their unqualified trust in any place, institution, ideological camp. Interestingly, Simone Weil's thinking hovers over this correspondence, especially Milosz's share of it, though Merton, too, has made her acquaintance with obvious relish. She, too, strenuously denounced Soviet totalitarianism early in the 1930s, when others of the French intelligentsia were all too accepting and excusing of it—yet she could be relentlessly, penetratingly Marxist (or materialistic) in her analysis of the fate of France's workers or, more broadly, the political struggle taking place in Europe before the onset of the Second World War. For her, life is bound by "necessity"—a way of giving full credit to the materialism that defines us significantly, no matter the philosophical and psychological efforts of some to ignore such matters as class and caste, with all that goes with those words, nation by nation. Still, she would break free, at least somewhat, of such an ironclad determinism, would embrace Jesus and (in a qualified way) the Catholic Church: the "light" that in her dualistic scheme of things occasionally broke into a world of darkness. For her the words "gravity and grace" (the phrase so arresting, even lyrical) described our condition: the heavy fatefulness of this life—though Jesus did come to us, and as well, the Greek thinkers whose ideas and language she so much respected, loved.

No wonder Milosz, like Camus, looked up to her so much, called upon her constantly, even visited her mother when he was living outside Paris; and no wonder Merton wanted to pursue her writing ever more seriously. She herself had a dramatic, rebellious mind; for the morally demanding minds of others, she could be a source of enormous stimulation, satisfaction—the brisk back-of-the-hand she kept giving to any number of secular pieties, even as she so obviously aligned herself with the world's humble people whose daily circumstances she came to know firsthand as a factory worker, agricultural laborer. At times there was a prideful fussiness to her, an insistence on being a scold, an inclination that occasionally turned into an eagerness to call for a plague to descend on both sides in this or that struggle—and I suspect in that regard she could only be inviting to Milosz, who saw clearly the horror of Soviet totalitarianism (and described those evils in *The Captive Mind*), but who had little use (we learn in these letters) for the Western materialism so many of us simply accept as inevitable, if not desirable. She belongs to Irving Howe's "homeless left," which would include Orwell, Silone, Danilo Dolci. Merton, though, like Dorothy Day, had a home in the Catholic Church, and, again like her, he was far from comfortable with the historical relationship of some of its leaders to the rich and powerful of various countries.

As one reads this epistolary novel of sorts (two characters in search of a moral vision), one realizes how many secular gods have failed—not just the murderous Communism, whose extravagant promises enchanted for a while so many of the intelligentsia. Merton and Milosz find common ground in their skepticism—the distance they put between themselves and faddish cultural or intellectual trends. Milosz scorns the French theorists who have come to mean so much in certain precincts of American university life, does so with the unashamed vigor and confidence of one who has no need to prove his intellectual credentials through a showy adherence to murky and far from modest theory-making; and Merton dares take on with tough, fearless candor his own "monastic life [where] there is a fatal mixture of inspiration and inertia that produces an awful inarticulate guilt in anyone who does not simply bury his head in the sand." The feisty clearheadedness of these two pilgrims, and their persistent self-scrutiny, become for the reader a sacred gift, but also a prod: how to follow their lead, hold to a similar skepticism, when warranted, while nevertheless pursuing with resolve moral principles, spiritual truths?

*Like a Hebrew prophet, Erikson was insisting upon
psychological investigation as a moral calling.*

During the late 1960s the psychoanalyst Erik H. Erikson taught an immensely popular undergraduate course at Harvard College. He used some of his own suggestive, edifying essays, but he also encouraged those of us who helped him teach as section leaders to use novels such as *Invisible Man*, or short fiction, such as Flannery O'Connor's "Everything That Rises Must Converge," "The Displaced Person," "The Lame Shall Enter First." We'd meet with him every week to talk about the way things were working out in the class, and often we'd wander in our discussions—take advantage of the privileged opportunity we had to be with him for a couple of hours by putting questions to him, thereby telling him of our various interests and concerns.

We kept addressing the subject of psychoanalysis in those discussions—its nature and purpose, of course, but also its relationship to a secular culture in which it had so obviously prospered. Erikson would remind us repeatedly of the irony—that a nation Freud himself both misunderstood and disliked (probably the former accounting for the latter) had become the virtual homeland of his discipline, the country where it was most fully accepted and where the majority of its practitioners did their work. Not that we had a hard time speculating on the reasons for that development. We kept on mentioning the materialism that prevailed in America—the preoccupation so many of us have with "goods and services," with ownership of various kinds, and, not least, with ourselves as a commodity of sorts: our appearance, our presentation of ourselves as decisive matters in determining our personal, social, and even occupational destiny.

I can still hear Erikson helping us walk through such a level of thinking; I can still remember his pointed, penetrating comments as he did so. "You have to remember," he once told us, "that Freud was using psychoanalysis to learn more and more about the mind, not to help his patients 'adjust' to society." Another time, he made the following observation, drawing on his own experiences as a young member of the so-called "Freud circle" in Vienna in the late 1920s and early 1930s: "Back then, psychoanalysis was attractive to a lot of us who were rebellious, unwilling to settle for the status quo. Now, especially here [in America], it draws upon different candidates [aspirants for training]."

He told us, in that regard, to go look up an important address Anna Freud had just given (in 1968) at the New York Psychoanalytic Institute—and I obligingly did so. She had, indeed, reminded her listeners that a profession once meant to challenge all sorts of psychological and social notions of what is and ought to be had in a generation become very much the property of an upper-bourgeois world, its inhabitants thoroughly interested in maintaining their hold on power, authority, wealth. Face to face with her audience of attentive colleagues, she dared compare their situation as successful, much respected psychoanalytic psychiatrists with the "disbelief, the ridicule, the suspicions, and the professional ostracism to which the first generation of analysts were exposed." She called those early colleagues of her father's "pioneers," reminded those in attendance at that Eighteenth Freud Anniversary Lecture that their predecessors had "ignored the conventional restrictions of their time," had been willing to risk "their social and professional status," and, "last but not least, in many instances gave up secure and profitable careers for financial uncertainties and hardship."

Those words were a blunt challenge to a particular entrenched institutional life. Moreover, those words were not unlike the ones used by Erikson, her onetime analysand, in his epilogue to *Childhood and Society*, wherein he warns his readers that a psychoanalyst has to learn how to "discard archaic rituals of control," learn a humane rationality, but above all, "set free in himself and in his patient that remnant of judicious indignation without which a cure is but a straw in the changeable wind of history." Like a Hebrew prophet of the Old Testament, Erikson was insisting upon psychological investigation as, ultimately, a moral calling—otherwise, doctors and patients alike become all too pointlessly self-absorbed; and as the historian Christopher Lasch put it, they (we) slip into a "culture of narcissism."

As we mulled over such matters, Erikson was quick to remind us that not only medical or cultural institutions depart from their original mission, become the victims of success. "Think of the early Christians," he urged us, "and see what now passes in the name of the religion they fought so hard to establish." Not a pleasant assignment, many of us thought that day—and still do: from the perils and possibilities of marginality to the self-assurance that goes with a historically consolidated acceptance. No wonder we are told (warned) in the New Testament that "the last shall be first, the first last." What we can see before our eyes with respect to a medical subspecialty (the accommodation of a radical critique of our mental life to prevailing "principalities and powers") has happened again and again in the history of Christianity: in its early years, obviously, but in the course of more recent centuries, as well—the attrition of reformist energy, its all too regular defeat at the hands of those who run things in this world. "We're so busy trying to get along," Erikson pointed out, sighing deeply, "that we go along." He was talking about the surrender of a kind of combative idealism to the all too often touted virtue of practicality. But it wasn't hard for him, or us in his company, to remember how that trajectory has also characterized the institutional life of religions, political parties, universities: the pull of a special (sacred) moment, undercut by the countervailing tug of what gets called (secular) "reality."

*"The Third Reich was a product of German history,
but it was not the only possibility open to the country
at that time."*

Again and again in *Middlemarch* George Eliot warns against our inclination to be "theoretic," to embrace various absolutes, to lose thereby our sense of life's complexities, the ironies and paradoxes that inevitably present themselves to us, the fatefulness of things, the role of accident and incident ("circumstance," as she puts it) in shaping our destiny—be it that of individuals or nations. But it is in our nature to be tempted by generalizations of our own making, by formulations in which we invest everything we've got. Our egoism, our yearnings for power and authority, our understandable wish to live forever through our ideas—these become for others laws or a received truth.

For some of us, still interested in a biblical way of seeing the mind's activity, such a faith in theory, such a disposition to turn concepts or constructs into reifications, such a yen for determinisms (be they social, biological, political, economic, historical, psychological) tells of our boundless ambitiousness, our wish to be, as it were, larger than life, godlike—our ideas become ideologies, our words worshipped.

In the first story of the Old Testament, Adam's headlong, heedless pursuit of "knowledge" defined him (and us): original sin. Since then we have continued to show one another how much we want to know, can know, have come to know—to the point that time seems our only real problem. Over the years that become decades, centuries, all that is elusive, enigmatic, hard to figure, will yield to our explorations first, then to our conclusive categorizations. No wonder Flannery O'Connor observed that "the task of the novelist is to deepen mystery, and mystery is a great embarrassment to the modern mind."

The above line of thought kept crossing my mind recently as I read a book titled *Hitler's Thirty Days to Power*, which tells of what happened in January 1933, during those last critical days of the Weimar Republic. I had long believed that there was something inevitable about Hitler's assumption of dictatorial control over Germany, that for a combination of political and cultural reasons, not to mention his own charismatic brilliance and ruthlessness, he had become by the early 1930s hard if not impossible to stop—a man who had maneuvered his way to the top and awaited the fall of one or another last obstacle so that he could become chancellor. But Henry Ashby Turner Jr., a professor of history at Yale, tells quite another story in this book—and by its end the reader is face to face with the kind of uncertainty and indeterminacy that makes so many of us nervous as we contemplate human affairs. On January 1, 1933, we are reminded, Hitler was on the brink of losing everything he once thought he had a chance of gaining. His National Socialist Party had suffered a major defeat in the last election; the devastated German economy seemed, finally, ready for an upturn; and the president of the nation, the old general and war hero Paul von Hindenburg, in his eighties, had as much contempt as ever for Hitler and the Nazi thugs who accompanied him on his never-ending circuit of hate—one stop after another given to speeches fueled with the hysteria of prejudice—a source of satisfaction for some who were socially down on their luck, for others who were psychologically vulnerable. Yet four weeks and two days later Hitler had been summoned to the president's office, given the chancellorship—and the rest is the twentieth-century disaster we all know, or ought to know and never forget.

To read Professor Turner's chronicle is to go back in time, to hold one's breath as the world itself (its decent side) hangs in the balance—to hope against hope that somehow the then-chancellor, Kurt von Schleicher, would prevail in his earnest efforts to rescue a badly wounded economy. All the while, of course, one knows what will happen—even as a historian's narrative gifts keep one very much interested and constantly instructed.

In a last, Tolstoyan meditation on history ("Determinacy, Contingency, and Responsibility") that belongs to the speculative tradition of the long, reflective epilogue on the last pages of *War and Peace*, Turner makes clear the role of luck, good and bad, in the fortunes of Hitler, not to mention the rest of us who still have to consider what his rule meant—that one of the great, so-called "civilized" nations could make a mockery of that adjectival description of it, and that a campaign of gutter hate could eventually enlist the support, in one rationalized form or another, of the philosopher Martin Heidegger, the literary critic Paul de Man, the psychoanalyst Carl Jung, the poet Ezra Pound, not to mention thousands of doctors, lawyers, professors, and, yes, clergymen.

"An examination of the events of January 1933 undercuts notions of determinacy by revealing strong elements of contingency in the chain of events that brought Hitler to power," Turner observes. He continues: "The Third Reich was unquestionably a product of German history, but it was not the only possibility open to the country at that time. . . . The future dictator was rescued from failure only by a series of unpredictable developments over which he had no control."

Those thirty days deserve a playwright's command of dramatic exposition: millions of lives hanging in the balance, a collective chorus wailing in anticipatory lamentation, as certain evil protagonists, wrapped in the clothes of respectability, and even religion (Franz von Papen the worst, most culpable, among them) maneuver and maneuver and maneuver, their souls soaked in lies, vanity, malice, arrogance—and soon enough, the deluge, the crematoria, the stacks of bones, Conrad's "heart of darkness" situated not near an obscure river of a distant, colonized continent, but in the drawing rooms and dining rooms and book-lined studies of an "advanced" nation's *haute bourgeoisie*.

Surely someone would come by, see me standing there
helplessly, offer a phone or a lift.

One evening several years ago, as dusk was settling in, I felt the car I was driving homeward become wobbly and hard to control. I pulled my car to the side, got out, and soon enough realized that I had a flat tire. I'm not very good with my hands, and each second, darkness was gaining its complete victory. I put on the lights, found the equipment meant to help me change tires, but I was soon enough engulfed by anxiety and fear. I'd never be able to do the job right; I'd be there forever; it was getting cold. Rhetorical questions kept posing themselves—why didn't I carry a cellular phone in the car, and why didn't I trade the car in last spring (the ruminative laments of the American upper-bourgeoisie)? I also began to despair of ever being able to make the switch of tires successfully there, then—and so, new questions: Ought I get back in the car, drive it, no matter the flat, until I get to a gas station, or ought I walk or drive to a home, knock on the door, and ask to use a phone to summon AAA?

Meanwhile, I tried my best to get the car lifted, so that I could start undoing bolts, then remove the wounded tire and replace it with the spare. But I was getting no place fast. I couldn't get the gadget meant to elevate the car to work, try and try as I did. Finally I stood up and walked a few steps away from the car—all too aware of the frustration, irritation, apprehension threatening to overcome me. I started noticing cars go by. They were nice cars, new or relatively new, driven by my fellow burghers. Many of them, I knew, had cellular phones, and some even faxes. I recalled a scene I'd witnessed a few days earlier, as I inched out of my hometown on the way to work—a man in his car taking an occasional slurp of coffee, then making a phone call, then reading what I assumed to be a fax that he pulled from a machine within arm's length. All the while his left hand, please God, held the steering wheel of his Mercedes-Benz—the day's important work already begun! Surely someone like him would come by, see me standing there helplessly, stop to offer a phone or a lift to a place where a phone was to be had.

But the cars kept whizzing by, their assured capability a second-by-second reminder of my needy vulnerability, not to mention my mechanical incompetence. I stood there, watching the steady, unrelenting approach of those cars and their fast disappearance into the night. I decided to go back into my car, get warmed up a bit, and drive to the next house in hopes of being allowed the hospitality of entrance, the use of a phone.

Just as I was going to get into my car I saw yet another pair of lights approaching—only this time, they didn't swiftly pass me by. My car and I were soon bathed in the steady, illuminating beam from what turned out to be a small truck weighed down by boxes. The vehicle came to a full stop. A tall burly man, with no sweater or jacket despite the chilly weather, stepped out. He wore a work shirt and dungarees. From the side of his mouth dangled a cigarette, which he removed and held in his hand—not the kind of well-to-do commuter who mostly used that road, I thought. Then this: "Is everything all right?" As I gathered myself for a reply, I realized how evasive, if not suspicious I felt. Who was he—why had he stopped, with what intent? Tersely I replied, "I got a flat." Had a different kind of person in a big, fat BMW stopped, a phone antenna discreetly placed in the rear, I can only imagine how smiling and effusive (and self-pitying, with an eye toward ingratiation in hopes of help) I'd have been. Instead, I was standing back, holding back—reluctant to get myself into more trouble, so I thought. But the man was hearty, cheerful, talkative. He asked me if he could be of help. "These things always happen at the wrong place, at the wrong time," he lamented. He was "pretty good at fixing flats," he let me know, with enough of a mumble to attest to his modesty. It was then that I relaxed, told him I was "no good" at what he claimed some ability to do—and then, his offer to "go at it," a phrase I liked as much as what I saw him accomplish, I swear, in about five minutes at the outside.

As he wiped his hands with a rough-edged piece of cloth he had in his rear pocket (I thought of the handkerchief in my own pants, all clean and ironed), I wondered how to thank him, what to do, and, yes, what to give. Some money—a gesture of gratitude? Ask for his address to send him "something"? But I realized how insulting (and actually, ungrateful) my mind was allowing me to be. I reached for his hand, gave him the heartiest of thanks. We gabbed for a few minutes. Some rock music had been playing in his truck all the time, and we talked of it. Then he told me he had to "get up and go," and he did. So did I—into the darkness and, as I thought then, maybe into yet another precinct of Conrad's "heart of darkness" as well—all those Mercedes-Benzes and BMWs and Volvos, with my confident kind in them at the big-shot wheels.

*I was witness to the moral energy a painter or
photographer can stir in children.*

As a volunteer teacher of elementary school children, I have for many years brought to class transparencies to show the boys and girls the work of great artists, illustrators, and photographers. Although my primary function has been to teach English to children from hard-pressed families, I have learned that sometimes a picture projected on a screen can do wonders for the imagination, can prompt both reflection and conversation—after which the children almost invariably write more spirited, forceful compositions.

I had an especially satisfactory time one morning with Winslow Homer's work, two segments of which I brought to the attention of the class: his school pictures, done in the early 1870s (*Country School, The Noon Recess, Snap the Whip*) and his efforts to render African American life in the South in the late 1870s (*The Cotton Pickers, Sunday Morning in Virginia, A Visit from the Old Mistress*).

These city children were surprisingly interested in the America of yore that Homer presents: the one-room school, the unblemished, inviting rural landscape, the evident outdoor fun enjoyed at recess by the children. But from nine- and ten-year-olds I heard some interesting questions:

"There are only a few kids around," one girl pointed out, adding: "They all look alike, so what will they hear from each other that they don't already know?" Much poignant and ironic discussion on that score in this class, which had no white students.

Several children remarked on the teacher in *The Noon Recess*. She seems "sad," the children thought, "alone" or, at a minimum, lost in her own thoughts ("She's thinking about something that might be worrying her"). A boy near the teacher is intent on reading, while outside his classmates frolic; and the children in my class wonder whether the youngster oughtn't to put aside his book, try to draw out "that lady, because she looks like she needs company." I'm much interested in that line of conversation, because it enables us, by indirection, to talk about moral and psychological authority—the necessary barriers between adults and young people, but also the desirability of trust and candor. "You should respect the teacher, and if she wants to have her thoughts, then you should let her be; but maybe a kid, every once in a while, can help out a grown-up, if she's got herself some trouble, by lending an ear"—a girl's tenderly reflective summation that gives us pause and settles the matter, at least temporarily.

Soon enough we'd be taking up the question of power and deference in another way—through Homer's confrontation between former slaves and their onetime mistress. Everyone in the class stared at the picture long and hard. None of them had ever been asked to approach that subject through contemplation of a picture, even though they'd been studying American history and knew well that the Emancipation Proclamation, issued in 1863, was a mere beginning in the struggle of African American people to obtain a host of rights and privileges others had all along been able to take for granted. The children are eager to put themselves emotionally in the shoes of both the dignified, well-dressed "old mistress" and the blacks of all ages before her, a grandmother sitting, two women standing, one with a child in her arms. They wonder how those recently freed Americans felt toward this onetime owner of theirs—and I hear in the surmises of the boys and girls that mix of awe and anxiety, deference and defiance, fear and fury that the powerful have inspired among the weak in many places and times.

Homer, of course, was a brilliantly original artist and had no need of words; he simply placed two worlds side by side and left the contemplation to us, his viewers. But it is to his credit that such a scene is ours to absorb, ponder—as the children realize: "Cool, that he went south and looked around!" (I had given the class some biographical information about the painter's documentary expeditions during the middle 1870s.) Moreover, I was more than a little surprised by the willingness of my school children, either African American or Latino in background, to speculate, with no little exertion of charity, about the "mistress," her sense of things, the emotions of her heart as she stood there, face to face, as it were, with history, hers and our nation's. "She must have felt bad. She came to see them, didn't she? Maybe she had to—she couldn't sleep at night, remembering . . ." Others picked up after the boy who spoke those words abruptly stopped—told us of the "horrible things" that "mistress" probably had in mind in the middle of the night and reminded us of the long hours of work done by slaves so that their masters and mistresses could live so well.

We looked at another of Winslow's paintings, *The Cotton Pickers*, which shows two young black women carrying their harvest. On a more upbeat note, we looked, too, at an early Homer masterpiece, *Sunday Morning in Virginia*, with its young blacks intently absorbed in reading, while an elderly black woman, unable to read, stares into space.

Immediately, the children got Homer's point (the hope literacy offers), but in an unforgettable gesture of empathy, they extended themselves toward the elderly woman, worried about her. They remarked upon her patience, her pleasure (so they saw it) in what her children and grandchildren were doing, learning. Once again I was a witness to the moral energy that a painter or photographer can stir in children. I fear that many of us in America's schools don't quite do justice to the educational and moral possibilities of such visual moments in our classrooms.

There is hope in those sudden, unexpected,
breakthrough experiences that bring us a blessed
spell of inwardness.

A s Kierkegaard reminded his Danish fellow burghers (in "The Present Age") and as his talented twentieth-century American disciple, Walker Percy, more than hinted in *The Moviegoer* (for all its humor, a deadly serious novel), we often get lost not through big moral missteps but as a consequence of life's everydayness become a thick, blinding fog. Absorbed by things to do, places to go, purchases to make, we stop asking what it is that matters and forsake moral consciousness in favor of a host of routines, felt social or pecuniary compulsions, all the supposed privileges of a bourgeois life. Still, there is hope for any of us—those sudden, unexpected, breakthrough experiences that come upon us, bring us up short, bring us to our senses, bring us a blessed spell of inwardness, of distance from the clatter and chatter, the hurry and the hustle of what gets called a normal or busy life.

A fax came to me the other day from a teaching colleague, a busy mother of three young children, a most conscientious guide for her students, a loyal and caring wife, and for all that, a civic-minded citizen who meets with others in a New England town library to discuss novels and short stories. I was told some academic news in the message—the usual bureaucratic details that the head section person in a course needs to let the professor know. At the end, though, I learned of a parent's headlong rush, day after day, to stay ahead of her family's needs, requirements, requests, worries, and apprehensions—"racing down grocery aisles, racing to head off a child's accident [a son has just learned to walk, and the stairs are nearby], racing to keep pace with all the dishes being cooked on the stove, racing to answer the phone, the doorbell, racing to get a fax or now to send one, to get to the nursery school on time, to do this and that and the next thing"—to be there, be there, be there for her family, her students, her colleagues, her friends and neighbors. But I also learned of a pause in all that motion, that constant expenditure of psychological and physical energy, a brief but big pause: "I stopped in my tracks when I heard Nicholas finish [reciting] the alphabet: Z, he said, and then he was quiet, pleased with himself but still his shy self. I was pleased, too—pleased that he'd gotten all the letters right and pleased with the composed, unassuming way he had of being pleased." For a few seconds, she was aware of what a miracle this life is, the miracle of language, the miracle of modesty, and the miracle of meaning, when you find it in a moment.

Just before that I had read a poem titled "Mysticism for Beginners," by the great Polish writer Adam Zagajewski. The poem offers lessons learned by watching this life carefully. The narrator had noticed someone holding a small book on his lap, titled *Mysticism for Beginners*, and he is prompted to reflect, remember, and "understand." He recalls "swallows patrolling the streets" of a city, "with their shrill whistles," and "the hushed talk of timid travelers," like himself in Europe's eastern countries, and "the white herons standing . . . like swans in fields of rice," and the way dusk can erase the distinctiveness of a particular landscape and "the little nightingale practicing its speech beside the highway." These and other visual recollections are his mind's response to that phrase "Mysticism for Beginners." He gives us brief but ever so suggestive and telling glimpses of eternity's scheme of things, moments of occurrence, be it that of human beings going their various ways or nature exerting itself—infinity's unfolding—the vastness of space and time and energy become concrete, there for us to apprehend, consider, and take to heart (rather than, alas, let slip by unnoticed, unsavored).

In his great moral fable, "The Housebreaker of Shady Hill," John Cheever has the story's protagonist, Johnny Hake, let himself into his suburban neighbor's home, which he knew well, so that he could make off with a wallet full of cash, a middle-of-the-night theft prompted by a notice of impending job loss. Cheever dares strip him morally and psychologically, this highbred resident of one of our twentieth-century American favored communities. Hake is revealed to himself rather than noticed, caught by others. In a climactic moment of self-awareness he walks the streets, then heads homeward by train; and so doing, he is touched by grace, a consequence of a humility quite new to him: "It seemed to me fishermen and lone bathers and grade-crossing watchmen and sand-lot ballplayers and lovers unashamed of their sport and the owners of small sailing craft and old men playing pinochle in firehouses were the people who stitched up the big holes in the world, that were made by men like me."

A mother's contemplation of the daily, a poet's ironic sensibility, insistent upon seeing the concreteness of awe and wonder and mystery, a storyteller's hymn to the ordinary as, finally, the (morally) exceptional—these are the revelations granted us on this wayfarer's journey of ours, as both Kierkegaard and Percy were anxious for themselves, for us, their readers and grateful students, to keep in mind. How well I remember Dorothy Day, a book in hand by Gabriel Marcel, whose humane philosophical writing she dearly loved, saying: "I hope this [a nod to the book she carried] will help me pay attention to God's gifts—the elderly couple holding on for dear life as they pass by, the hungry people we serve at meal-time, the tree outside our door, all by itself making such a difference to those sparrows, and to us, too, if we'd only stop to know it."

This double standard could all too readily be accommodated by the slippery imprecisions of psychiatric jargon.

Before the Vietnam War prompted many to have grave reservations about military service, most young physicians had to give two years to the army, navy, or air force under the provisions of what used to be called the "Doctors' Draft." (Now our armed forces train their own doctors or make arrangements to pay the tuition of certain medical students in exchange for their later obligation to serve.) Because I'd had some psychiatric and psychoanalytic training, I was put in charge of an air force psychiatric service in Biloxi, Mississippi—yet another military doctor counting each day of his two-year stint and regarding it as an unwelcome interlude, at best. In retrospect, however, I've come to realize how very much I owe to that time spent at Keesler Air Force Base. For one thing, I'd never before been in the South, and it was as a resident of Mississippi in 1960 that I came to witness the struggles of black children (in nearby New Orleans, which I often visited) to integrate hitherto all-white schools.

My whole life thereupon changed. I never did rush back to New England at the end of my military assignment. Indeed, even during it I had begun to make the kind of inquiries that would characterize all my later work—interviews (in homes and in schools) with children and their families who were caught in one or another social or political or moral struggle. In a sense, then, an air force assignment which I initially regretted (how much better to serve in a European military hospital, or one on the West Coast or Asia!) turned out to be a shaping influence upon my occupational life—the kind of irony the novelist George Eliot urged us to appreciate: fate and chance and circumstance as powerful aspects of our destiny, determinants all too commonly overlooked these days in favor of those tossed our way by various social scientists, who so often are on the lookout for psychological or sociological theories that explain anything or everything all too unequivocally.

But apart from an accidental encouragement to one doctor's future research, that air force hospital kept giving many of us physicians plenty of pause—to the point that we frequently talked of the "education" we were receiving as we struggled to reconcile our professional (really, moral) values with the various policies sent our way through the military chain of command. We noticed, for instance, that when we regarded enlisted men and women who drank a lot or who were struggling with various sexual problems (struggling hard, many of them, to figure out who they were, so to speak—the matter of "orientation" or "preference," as it is put in psychiatric lingo), we were mindful of the desires of our superiors to "board them out administratively"—i.e., to discharge such men and women as having "character disorders" and hence as not fit for service, and hence with no future rights as veterans, not to mention with a mark of suspicion in the eyes of future employers. With officers it was quite another matter. We were asked to be more than considerate and kind; we were asked to mobilize a psychiatric vocabulary for the purpose of strengthening (rather than undermining) the reputation of these individuals—so that they could be kept in the service, if possible, or if not, honorably discharged with full benefits.

This informal but distinct double standard could all too readily be accommodated by the slippery imprecisions of psychiatric jargon, by a profession's inevitable subjectivity. In Tillie Olsen's hauntingly powerful story "Hey Sailor, What Ship?" a mother tells the following to her daughter (who has been denouncing a longtime family friend, a lowly, hard-drinking seaman): "I care you should understand. You think Mr. Norris is a tragedy. You feel sorry for him because he talks intelligent and lives in a nice house and has quiet drunks." The daughter had been contemptuously throwing around the word "wino" in just the way we were urged to use the language of psychopathology with pejorative intent when we made our decisions about the privates and corporals entrusted to us. For our Mr. Norrises (and there were no small number of them) another tone altogether was wanted, a medical slant that favored the kind of "understanding" Olsen's mother wants for a sailor. Put differently, and with all too brutal terseness, we were learning as young doctors in the military that class most significantly can affect medical decisions.

Not that we didn't resist, say no, try to uphold what we considered a fair and decent regard for all the men and women we saw in that military hospital. But the pressures of a bureaucracy can be powerful, the temptation strong to bury worries and misgivings in a tide of rationalizations and self-justifications. Anyway, we were there for only a couple of years, and our objections could be circumvented, we knew, by the savvy persistence of the majors and lieutenant colonels and colonels who had no hesitation to lord it over us in many ways. I don't want to say that we abjectly surrendered, that we didn't try to stand firm for our convictions. Nevertheless, we often came back to that story of Olsen's, which had been published a few years earlier (1957), and in our angrier moments, to Salinger's *The Catcher in the Rye*, with its mantra about "phoniness" and its assault on institutional pretensions and deceits, as we tried to uphold our ideals in our lived professional lives, even as we made those adjustments of attitude and action (maybe even of conscience) that get subsumed, alas, under that catch-all word "practicality." So it often goes, I suspect, and not only among those in the military. We keep deferring in various ways to money, position, power—not quite what the Hebrew prophets and Jesus Christ had in mind for us to do.

The doctor who is sick now turns his students into the kind of physician he himself has been with others.

A friend of mine from medical school, now an internist in St. Louis, recently sent me a videotape of a meeting between his brother, also a physician, and some first-year students at Washington University's School of Medicine. The students are there to talk with a longtime, much-revered doctor and teacher who (they know) is suffering from an incurable cancer that is well on its way to claiming full victory. Even so, this afflicted man in his sixties looks well for his age; he has a full head of dark brown hair that shows no sign of graying, and he is in fit shape. On the other hand, as he talks it is clear that he can't take breathing for granted—and, of course, the telltale sign not only of his distress, but his vulnerability, his jeopardy, is a plastic tube wrapped around his head, which supplies him with much-needed oxygen.

Soon enough, we learn that this hardworking, conscientious, and sensitive physician, who for many years attended hundreds of patients with great care and much medical success, had diagnosed his own disease—cancer of the lung, even though he was a nonsmoker. We meet him well into that illness—symptomatic but ambulatory, to slip into clinical language. He is a forceful, insistent teacher eager to conduct a seminar, and his students are very much the composed yet eager young men and women who nowadays attend our medical schools: hugely privileged (the competition for admission is fierce, statistically staggering) but restrained by their obvious realization of how very much they have to learn, no matter their previous proven abilities.

At first the discussion is conventionally academic: the old comparison of coronary heart disease and cancer—the former with its often quick conclusion, the latter so commonly relentless. The teacher observes wisely but with a clinician's detachment that a sudden, fatal coronary seizure can be hard for families—no time to say good-bye to someone who has unexpectedly expired. In contrast, cancer can be terribly demanding on those who suffer from it (the day-by-day awareness of a finality that won't be deterred), though the patient's kin do get a chance to come to terms gradually with the prospect of approaching death. Soon enough, however, the students and the teacher are no longer talking in the abstract but concretely: how does this person, the man before them, manage these days—he who is steadily and surely losing the battle for his earthly existence.

Now the voice tightens, the body becomes more mobile, the words pour forth with greater volume and urgency. We hear an alert, knowing teacher expound on the dying patient from both the doctor's point of view and the patient's. Hope matters, we are told—yet many cancers cannot be stopped. They are slow killers. Patients try hard to rid themselves of that kind of knowledge. The resort to "denial" (that word a banality of our time) is harder for a physician, especially one who is not prone to fancy or illusion. This doctor, a sensible, practical realist and a thoroughgoing rationalist, has seen through so much denial in his patients that it can't quite sustain its tempting hold on him—though he confesses to near-miss moments, when he was almost able to persuade himself that he wasn't so sick, after all, and that he was on the road to recovery. Moreover, "denial" isn't necessarily something to be condemned out of hand. An experienced internist reminds his students (and himself) that when patients begin to lose hope and see the end as around the corner, they lose ground physically, as if the body nods acquiescence to a despairing mind.

What to think, to feel, under such circumstances? This knowing healer of others, now himself going through a last illness, rejects a traditional religious point of view—an afterlife as propounded by biblical Christianity. He foresees his survival as a remembered person in the thoughts of his family, friends, patients, though he is sensible and sensitive enough to allow that the immediacy and intensity of those memories will yield to time's erosions—so that forgetfulness will inevitably bring him down, so to speak, a second time. All he can do, then, is talk the matter out—even as he tells his students that all they will be able to do, come their time as physicians, is hear out their future patients as they struggle with their dread of an exit from this human scene.

Irony has multiplied: The doctor who is sick now turns his students into the kind of physician he himself has been with others—they listen and listen as he talks and talks, ever more poignantly, insistently. At one point the camera catches a single tear rolling down the cheek of a medical student—an essential sadness given visual expression: a proudly stoic late twentieth-century American scientific materialism (with its psychoanalytic offshoot) acknowledged empathically in its terribly threatened presence. Within seconds the film is over and darkness comes to the screen, even as the viewer knows that darkness has already descended upon the doctor just shown—his "afterlife," as he has instructed us, a courtesy of us who choose to watch, to hold him in our thoughts. As I listened to the VCR clicking away, rewinding the tape, I realized I'd been offered one individual's appraisal of his place in eternity's scheme of things—a brave, uncompromising, unyielding statement of what dying means (and arguably, for any number of people, a bleak and scary one). No wonder many of us are glad to let our minds explore other possibilities—to see this time we are each given here from a different angle of vision.

Through the use of fictional strategies, the writer offers us a clue about oppression.

I n 1963 my wife, Jane, was teaching a fourth-grade class in Atlanta, Georgia. All her students were of African American background.

The South at the time was very much in the midst of social struggle and change. In fact, the two of us were then studying the progress of school desegregation in Atlanta, after observing an earlier version of it in New Orleans. One morning as the class was discussing American history, the Civil War in particular, a girl raised her hand, ostensibly to offer her take on the nature of and the reasons for Sherman's well-known "march through Georgia," which had taken place almost a century earlier. But instead she treated the class to a disquisition of sorts. She mocked those who have criticized that campaign as too cruel and destructive ("After all, it was a war they were fighting"); and she went further, wondering why Sherman's military behavior has become for some so notorious, whereas the everyday experience of slavery "doesn't get a lot of people upset," as she put it. Others in the class disputed that comparison. One girl made a racial distinction, observing that "it's white folks who worry about what Sherman did." She went further and told her fellow students the following: "Even for us colored people—how can you really know what it was

41

like being a slave? My momma, my grandma—they say it was so bad, you can't imagine how bad, so it's better you don't try."

I thought of that long-ago discussion, recorded in a teacher's journal my wife kept, as I recently read an extraordinarily powerful novel about an American family, first published in England four years ago under a title, *Theory of War*, that suggests a ponderous political science text. The novelist, Joan Brady, has chosen her own grandfather, Jonathan Carrick, as her story's protagonist; and she tells us about him in an author's note: "My grandfather was a slave. This isn't an uncommon claim for an American to make if the American is black. But I'm not black. I'm white. My grandfather was white, too. And he was sold into slavery not in some barbaric Third World country: he was sold in the United States of America. A Middle Western tobacco farmer bought him for $15 when he was four years old; not many people knew about such sales, although they were common just after the Civil War."

The book makes sure that more of us will know what it means for a child to grow up as the legally and socially sanctioned property of people who aren't parents, but rather owners—willing, therefore, to demand, insist, deny, and punish not out of love or concern or respect, but in the tradition of the market's brute calculations. To some extent the writer has given us a social history of our country's nineteenth-century prairie life; she has also summoned the tape recorder as an instrument of remembrance, and parts of her narrative are devoted to "oral history," to her determined effort to learn of her grandfather through the recalling voice of his physician son, Atlas, who was her uncle. Moreover, she keeps invoking the military strategist and essayist Karl von Clausewitz, who understood that war is a test of will (and desperation) as well as a matter of arms wielded.

Clausewitz is the reigning thinker of this chronicle because the author wants us to think of the consuming bitterness that arbitrary subjection and humiliation can prompt. This is a novel about America's westward expansion—about saloons and whorehouses and the building of railroads, about farming and the weather that makes it or breaks it, about a version of populism that took hold in small towns across the land. But the novel is really a psychological autopsy of a man who was, as a young child, stripped of his human rights and who eventually would run away from his callous and cruel masters. But he could not get them out of his head.

Slavery, we are meant to learn, won't so easily yield to new circumstances, be they the favorable accidents or incidents of life or even the achieved successes that hard work and applied intelligence can accomplish. In *Theory of War*, the protagonist's obvious agility of mind and body, his relentless determination to make a go of it, no matter the obstacles in his way, are not enough to placate his soul, to bring him the proverbial peace of mind that, in fact, will elude him all his life. Instead he is haunted by the past and driven to avenge it, so that only the murder of the son of his onetime bossman (that boy would eventually become a United States senator from Kansas) will bring a completion of sorts to this saga of enmity in search of expression and satisfaction.

I suspect that many of the well-educated, privileged, and white readers who will probably make up the majority of this book's readership will be moved to eager empathy with its terribly hurt central figure and will even find it possible to comprehend with compassion (if not to condone) his lasting rage, unsuccessfully countered by marriage, work, and parenthood. How much harder, though, for many of us to put ourselves in the shoes of the African Americans who still carry abiding grudges against those who enslaved them, against a nation that only a few decades ago was still plagued by segregationist laws, by an insistence upon race as a deciding measure of victory or defeat (to use the imagery of war), authority or vulnerability. Through the use of fictional strategies—by converting a family's history into an account that stirs the imagination, gives it permission to wander and wonder—the writer offers us a clue about oppression, its all too lasting consequences and the inevitable distance between those who have known it and those who merely hear or read of it.

*What appears to be bizarre and senseless is in many
cases a quite reasonable expression of horror.*

I n a previous column I made mention of my experiences as an air force
psychiatrist—the different ways we were expected to respond to our
fellow officers, as opposed to the ordinary men and women who hadn't
such high rank to their credit. Again and again some of us doctors, in the
military for only two years, were reminded that we had to accommodate
our notion of what ought to be to the requirements of a large organization
with its own traditions, customs, needs, and values.

Regeneration, a novel I recently read by Pat Barker, an Englishwoman,
brought back that military experience and reminded me of what was
often at stake as I first sat with people having trouble with their personal
lives and then sat with my fellow air force doctors as we tried to figure
out what to do, and why.

In the pages of *Regeneration* we are told of the terrible carnage of
the First World War—millions of young lives lost in senseless trench
combat over yards of territory drenched in blood. Three years into that
human and moral disaster the British poet and army officer Siegfried
Sassoon, a decorated war hero, abruptly refused to have any more part of
the fighting. His defiant challenge to military authority, called "A Soldier's

Declaration," is put at the beginning of the novel. At one point he insists: "I have seen and endured the suffering of the troops, and I can no longer be party to prolong these sufferings for ends which I believe to be evil and unjust."

Soon enough this well-known officer was a patient at Craiglockhart War Hospital, classified "mentally unsound." Such a procedure was supposedly a sign of early twentieth-century progress, an effort to understand rather than a quick punitive judgment.

At the hospital Sassoon became the patient of William Rivers, M.D., a neuropsychiatrist who even now is known to people in my profession as one of the pioneers in what came to be called the study of "war neuroses." He was one of the first doctors to take seriously the subjectivity of soldiers afflicted with all sorts of paralyzing symptoms: terrible nightmares, spells of deep gloom, appetite loss, insomnia, and a host of other idiosyncratic complaints that seemed to defy comprehension. He learned that what appears to be bizarre and senseless is in many cases a quite reasonable expression of horror on the part of men who had witnessed and experienced a degree of suffering and vulnerability unimaginable to those who have never been on a battlefield in, say, Ypres or Verdun, where corpses by the thousands covered land meant to grow crops, all in the name of this or that nation's "freedom" or "destiny."

Thanks to almost a century of psychoanalysis, we readily comprehend now how the mind tries to find symbolic expression for its grave distress, how the unconscious wields its way; but Dr. Rivers came to such knowledge on his own, through careful clinical observation and analysis and without resort to the sometimes ponderous and overwrought theoretical language of today that contrasts so markedly with the marvelously clear-headed and inviting narrative writing to be found in, say, Freud's *The Interpretation of Dreams.*

In fact, Dr. Rivers belongs to the tradition of British empiricism—a way of seeing things not unlike the approach to people and their behavior that William James, on this side of the Atlantic, called pragmatism. Indeed, had James lived another few years (he died in 1910), one suspects he would have been much interested in pursuing just the kind of inquiry Rivers made in his many encounters with so-called shell-shocked survivors of those hard-fought battles on French soil during the second decade of this century.

This is a chronicle that summons up a historical scene and probes it deeply, to the reader's considerable benefit. We learn what happens not only to hurt, war-weary soldiers, but to the doctors who must try to heal them—so that, alas, they will return to places of wanton slaughter as participants, as those who aim to kill, while hoping and praying they will themselves be spared. Fiction varies, of course, in its relationship to the actual and factual.

The account in this novel has obviously been made possible by the writer's long-standing and full immersion in historical sources of various kinds, as she readily acknowledges in an author's note at the end—a novel in the documentary tradition and an attempt to evoke through the strategies of the storyteller a long-ago medical and social reality: the psychiatric hospital as a place of twentieth-century military decision-making.

But the book is also informed by a moral seriousness not always explicitly acknowledged by some of us psychiatrists as we do our work, in civilian as well as military life. All too easily we may try to address our patients' complaints, the troubles that have brought them to us, while keeping ourselves at a distance from the moral turmoil that has so urgently confronted them.

Dr. Rivers knew that Sassoon's psychiatric hospitalization was a moral dodge for the military, for an entire culture: What to do when a brave soldier has serious second thoughts about a war he hitherto accepted as just and necessary? To call such a person sick is, of course, to concentrate on the singular rather than the general—to call individuals crazy rather than regard a nation as gone mad. Even in times of peace, moreover, there are those who question strenuously the way things are—and get called by many of us all sorts of psychological names.

In *Regeneration* we are asked to think not only of the protester's motives and actions, but also those of his doctors. It is, in fact, the moral agony of the psychiatrist, Dr. Rivers, that won't let go of us who read of him—probably because his dilemmas remind us of some of our own.

"I'm really sorry. I never should have opened the door without looking. . . . I was lost in thought. I wasn't thinking."

I was riding my bike not long ago along a road in the town where I live, braced by a clear sunny day with enough edge to it, in the form of cool weather, to make me feel especially glad that I could enjoy myself this way in a quiet New England setting. I was on my way to the post office. Not far from my destination, I began to slow down—and a good thing I did. A car door was suddenly flung open. I reflexively squeezed my handbrakes tight, only to find myself unavoidably colliding with the door. In no time I was on the road, the bike crashing down beside me.

Supine on the asphalt, I had a delightful view of the sky. My eye caught sight of a tree I'd passed for years and not noticed. Now it seemed like a handsome umbrella shielding the nearby sidewalk and cars. Abruptly I heard a voice, then saw its owner, a man who had been sitting in his car and decided to take leave of it just as I was approaching the part of the road where he was parked. I heard, "Oh, I'm so sorry—are you all right?" By then I was quite ready to test my limbs, my state of physical being. I was, as the expression goes, gathering myself together. I could use my legs and arms and torso in such a way that, thank God, I was able to stand up, even grab hold of my bike and stand it up. I took the two of us, my bike and me, to the safety of the sidewalk. Some considerate and, no doubt, alarmed drivers who had stopped in their tracks now gratefully proceeded.

I was neurologically and musculo-skeletally intact, or so it seemed— the doctor in me joining hands with the plain old human being in a second's smile of relief. Still, I felt vulnerable and sore (maybe in several senses of that word). I somehow didn't care whether I got to the post office. The couch in my study at home crossed my mind. I wanted to be there, dozing, to be miraculously transported there—enough of this bicycle business! I believe that, already, my back was telling me that it was going to commemorate this event, register pain, turn me into someone who has to watch his every move.

Meanwhile, as I stood there trying to get myself back into the swing of things, the man I'd seen hovering over me—who had pushed open the left front door of his Series 5 BMW right in time for me to greet it head on and meet its resistance, to which I quickly gave way in surrender—now stood before me, looking me up and down, staring at my bike. That became, in fact, the object of his solicitude: "Is it all right? Will it take you home, do you think?" I nodded; I couldn't muster the one affirmative word necessary. I moved the bike, though, back and forth—to tell by showing. Then came my turn for this fellow's show of interest: "I hope you're OK." I had no time to answer—more came forth: "I'm really sorry. I never should have opened the door without looking." Another very brief pause. Then: "I was lost in thought. I wasn't thinking. . . ."

At once the memory of my dear, English-born father came to my mind, with his habit of spotting inconsistencies in the spoken word, not to mention grammatical errors. He was a polite fellow, but he would have eventually remarked to me, had he been there, that this owner of a quite fine automobile, who lived in a comfortable town (and who was dressed in a suit and shirt and tie that looked as if they'd only recently been housed at Brooks Brothers) can't have everything. "Bobby," my dad would have said, "you can't be 'lost in thought' and 'not thinking' at the same time." My mom and later my wife, Jane, and even later our three sons, as they got older, would have had the necessary gumption, thank God, to respond, to tell him that logic doesn't always work as a means of approaching human affairs. For (as in this instance) one can most certainly be quite consumed by one's private thoughts, hence oblivious (in one's "thinking" life as a responsible citizen) to what was happening nearby and, so, unprepared to take a thoroughly necessary kind of action.

Anyway, my reverie over, I told this man that I was sorry too—sorry I'd come to that spot when I did, sorry I'd gotten me and my bike into this situation. Then a half-meant gesture of politeness on my part: "Is your car door all right?" "Oh yes," I was told; "those cars are *strong*."

Seconds later he was on his way. He'd offered his name and address, had begun to reach for his wallet, for a business card. "Oh, no," I averred. With a great display of my own strength (I can show those BMWs!), I moved on in a burst of speed to get my errands done, return home—where I rather quickly realized how painful my back was as I bent or moved too quickly. Still, I was not without a moral lesson: When we let self-absorption take over our lives, we can make others pay a stiff price (literally so in this case). Since I've many times been "where" that man was (all too self-preoccupied) I've now come to regard him a friend, maybe even a messenger from on high with a necessary warning.

*It was the old story of teachers who have a lot to learn
from their humble, yet knowing, students.*

For the past four years I have been meeting with teachers and
principals from across the country who work in Catholic schools,
mostly located in inner-city neighborhoods. Men and women,
African American and white and of Hispanic background, lay people and
members of one or another religious order, they are all trying exceedingly
hard to make a difference in the lives of children who, often enough, are
living at the very edge of things economically and psychologically. Nor
are these individuals all that well paid; their salaries, almost invariably,
are lower than what they'd receive if they taught in public schools. But
they are devoted to their Catholic faith as well as to their vocation as
teachers, to the point that they pay little attention to the clock as they go
about their daily tasks.

They come to Boston, twenty-five to thirty strong, as members of the
Summer Institute for Spiritual Growth at Boston College—two weeks of
discussions, lectures, churchgoing, more than occasional praying, trips to
Boston's plentiful cultural attractions, including a visit to Fenway Park,
where the Red Sox these days are a collective shadow, alas, of their earlier
selves, but where one can still have a great time.

I meet with the teachers for half a day twice each week. I ask them to read the stories of Tillie Olsen, collected under the title *Tell Me a Riddle*, and two stories by Raymond Carver, "A Small, Good Thing" and "Cathedral." I also suggest that they read a biography of Dorothy Day, and I've mentioned or used other short stories or novels or poems from time to time—moral fiction, mostly, that prompts a good deal of looking within, and that often stirs plenty of conversation. The institute fortunately has a shepherd in Mike Carrotta, of Louisville, Kentucky, who has worked with troubled youth, has been much involved in Catholic education and possesses a natural gift for bringing people together and helping them get the most out of each other. They all stay in a religious setting, and are, in no time, thoroughly relaxed—a big breather of sorts to people who are used to a busy, demanding time of it, often with no letup at all.

No question, these are quite humble folk, I've learned—each group arrives surprised that they've obtained an opportunity to stop and think about things; and each group is hungry, indeed, for "advice" from us secular "experts" of one kind or another. Not that they are averse to reading stories—a number of them, after all, teach English. But they are Americans—hence an evident, strong interest in the formulations and theories of contemporary psychology and sociology. Indeed, some of them come well-armed with the latest abstract notions of various social scientists and look forward, in a college setting, to further acquaintance with the confident language of, say, educational psychology or, in my case, child psychiatry and psychoanalysis.

In that regard, I can still hear the words spoken to me on the first day of the first year's institute (by a wonderfully conscientious and big-hearted man who was a youth worker in a tough ghetto neighborhood): "I'm really looking forward to learning a lot here—so I'll be able to do a better job with all the kids I'm trying to reach." He told me much about those youngsters: how hurt they are, and so how distrustful they can be, and sometimes how angry and self-destructive—a melancholy story that he seemed to carry on his shoulders constantly. Soon enough, I sensed his earnest hope that somehow our institute would make a big difference in his working life—provide him, as he put it to me, with "answers to a lot of questions." Yet, I was there, rather, to listen and learn and offer only the modest lessons of well-crafted, morally energetic fiction—which, alas, stresses ambiguity, complexity, irony, and paradox, not exactly the staples of our secular authorities who claim to know so much about "human development" or "the behavioral aspects of classroom management" (to borrow a phrase I had recently seen in a university catalog).

As I have sat with those men and women, I have marveled not only at what they are doing in their respective jobs, but at their capacity to get so very much out of the fiction that we discuss, the lectures they attend, even the recreation we have planned for them. They can take a short story I have taught college undergraduates or medical students or hospital residents for years and bring its meaning to a new level of intensity and poignancy for me and Mike Carrotta—and have the two of us shaking our heads in surprise, gratitude, even awe. It took Mike and me a good deal of time to realize that here were people who could bring a quite special outlook to our assignments—the breadth and depth of their inner lives, their daily experiences, however strenuous the challenge posed to them by the youngsters they taught, made for extraordinary responses to stories meant, anyway, to elicit the reader's ethical and spiritual inwardness.

Each year, I have wanted, finally, to let these men and women know how lucky I am to be with them, how much I have learned from them. They keep saying, generously, that the institute is of benefit to them, strengthens them as they return to their ever so vulnerable situations in the front lines of our nation's various social struggles. But Mike and I have left each of those summer institutes strengthened ourselves, mindful, indeed, of our own need for the kind of moral and spiritual energy they so evidently possess—the old story of teachers who have a lot to learn from their humble yet knowing students.

Dorothy Day spoke of the irony: "All that philosophical knowledge, and such a moral failure; such blindness— and worse—in a life."

The 100th anniversary of Dorothy Day's birth prompted many occasions of celebration, reflection, remembrance. On campuses, in the many "hospitality houses" wherein the Catholic Worker tradition is carried on, in churches and in newspapers and magazines (including *America*) she was evoked, discussed, even upheld as a possible saint—her oft-quoted refusal of the desirability of such a future designation notwithstanding. Not that the acclaim is now universal—just as during her lifetime she had plenty of critics, for one reason or another, both within and outside the Catholic Church, which became her spiritual home in the fourth decade of her life. Her unwavering pacifism, maintained even during the Second World War, when the devil himself seemed among us in the person of Hitler, was especially hard for many of us to comprehend or, more instinctually, to stomach. Moreover, she was politically (with Orwell and Ignazio Silone) an eligible member of Irving Howe's "homeless left." True, she had most certainly found a home in the church she loved so passionately—the great "labor" encyclicals (*Rerum Novarum* and *Quadragesimo Anno*) were her kind of applied faith—yet she knew well how hard it is even for earnestly devout Christians to avoid the blandishments of a secular, materialist world. And such a posture of resistance set her apart from all sorts of "principalities and powers," not least some of those in the Catholic Church.

In a sense, then, she was a loner within an institution she much loved, and now those who make up its officialdom will decide whether she will (ought to) have a special spiritual recognition. In that regard I am of two minds—I don't think Dorothy Day was kidding, or slyly disguising her thoroughly human egoism through modest disclaimers, when she shunned the suggestion of sainthood for herself. On the other hand, I agree heartily with those who emphasize the church's need—its constant search for a symbolic assertion of Christ's message as it took hold of lives, became affirmed, realized in their daily actions.

How well I recall a long afternoon at St. Joseph's House, the Catholic Worker building in New York City at 36 East First Street, in 1974. My wife had been ill, and we had received one letter after another from Dorothy Day, her heartfelt prayers a big boost, an inspiration. Now Jane was better, and I had come to say thank you, to have yet another conversation with someone I'd first met while a medical student and had since admired without letup. She was frail in body, but as feisty as ever in spirit. We talked, as always, about her great loves, Dickens and Dostoevski. I had been trying to get her to enjoy Walker Percy's fiction, but with no success. I had sent her *The Moviegoer,* which I love, but she hadn't taken to it at all. She politely excused her lack of interest or response as "generational," but I thought then, and still do, that she favored writers whose gift and mission it was to render storytelling justice to the poor and to Christ as their onetime (and all-time) companion. It was hard for her to extend herself, heart and soul, toward Binx Bolling, the clever stockbroker-protagonist of Percy's *The Moviegoer*—though she did take note of the moral shift in that novel toward the end, when Binx leaves a sophisticated, privileged New Orleans world for Biloxi, Mississippi, where his humble half-brother Lonnie is dying.

I tried to get her to discuss Kierkegaard, whose ideas Percy worked into that novel so brilliantly and engagingly—but with no success. She knew that Percy was also a Catholic convert; she wanted to become a fan, but again, she was "too old." In truth, I began to realize, she didn't find the intellectual background that informed *The Moviegoer* (not only the ideas of Kierkegaard, but those of Heidegger) all that congenial. She knew of Heidegger's unapologetic Nazism; and as we talked of him and of that (I fear I was trying to make some points), her eyes glazed a bit, and a sad look came upon her face. Then she spoke of the irony: "All that philosophical knowledge, and such a moral failure; such blindness—and worse—in a life." Then she almost seemed to turn on herself, not for saying what she had said (and very much wanted to say), but for failing to say more: "It's tempting to let the matter drop there—another giant with big ideas brought down by the truth of his life. But we're all tested that way, by whether we live up to what we preach. We should be sad for Heidegger, for all of us. Pray for him hard."

I'd never thought of praying for Heidegger—only figuring out (not so easy) what he had to say, and only discussing him, arguing about him or, yes, taking note of that terrible irony: all that high theory (about "being," no less) and such a wrongheaded collusion with Hitler's hate, never kept under wraps. I felt uncomfortable, maybe chastised. She sensed my disease. Graciously, she tried to meet me halfway, so to speak—she brought up Pascal, a philosopher whose ideas meant so very much to her, and we talked of his various *pensées*, how utterly modern they still are—and then some unforgettable fun: "Wouldn't it be something," she said, "if the church made Pascal a saint, and while it's doing that, Bonhoeffer as well, not for his ideas, his theology, but for his life, what he did in the name of Christ." A thin smile crossed her face, as she (ever the restless revolutionary dreamer, impatient with institutional customs and practicalities and realities) contemplated that: a Lutheran minister thus exalted in Rome.

In Othello *we meet a man of great dignity and refinement who is gradually undone.*

A friend and teaching colleague of mine recently persuaded me to re-read *Othello*, which he assigned in his class this autumn. I had not read the play since college, when I went through it hurriedly as one more assignment in a yearlong course devoted to Shakespeare. We read a play a week in the fall, one tragedy after another. We struggled mightily with words and phrases unknown to us, with hidden meanings to which the professor alone seemed privy, with a blur of intrigue and guile and deceit and conceit—to the point that we began to realize why one critic had called the greatest of playwrights a "learned geographer of the Inferno."

I still remember that comment, and it came back to me with special force as I contemplated Iago, obviously, but beyond him the entire thrust of *Othello*, which will always be a modern play, inasmuch as it confronts us with ourselves: the part of us that knows jealousy and envy, rivalry and greed, and, not least, ambition. In that regard, Shakespeare was, of course, intensely, knowingly "psychological" centuries before the social sciences appeared, with all the fanfare of a promised new kind of knowledge. Indeed, in his bones Shakespeare possessed a subtle human awareness that makes a mockery of the overwrought, reductionist theories all too many of us in contemporary psychiatry and psychoanalysis have embraced with no small amount of pride.

Nor is *Othello* without a penetrating sociology that, in fact, eludes a large number of us today as we grapple with matters of race and class earnestly and sometimes all too simple-mindedly—through resort to sweeping categorizations that do scant justice to the complexity of things. Othello the Moor is "different," a prefiguration, in one sense, of the racial outsider who has troubled, even haunted us in America. How, we all wonder, have blacks managed in a society that has been so often indifferent at best to their singular history and experience? What happens, we also have cause to ask, when individual blacks are immersed in the company of people who don't respect them, who begrudge them whatever achievements they have to their record? And, very important, what accounts for the attitude of white people toward those unlike them in appearance; what prompts racial hatred, and how does such an attitude influence the outlook (and yes, the performance at school and work) of those so rejected, scorned?

Ironically, a man of the English theater in 1603 has given us of today a chance to think about "race" in the broadest, deepest manner. In a sense, *Othello* presents us with a future America, where more and more blacks will be prominent, successful, powerful—and therefore objects of envy. Put differently, Othello the Moor is not an outcast by virtue of his skin's hue, but rather someone who stirs the passions of a lesser man whose "prejudices," ultimately, tell us about his humanity rather than his "racism." In 1964, in Canton, Mississippi, in the midst of a heated political discussion by civil rights activists, I heard one of them say this: "I suppose the day will come when we won't be hated because we're black, but because of what we as individuals have done, or because of the kind of person we are."

I thought of that remark as I turned the pages of *Othello*—for in that dramatic narrative we meet a man of great dignity and refinement who is gradually undone not by virtue of racist terror but by his own vulnerabilities, all too human, as these are cleverly exploited by a person who is smitten by a desire to have what someone else has. Iago's demonic side is not that of a monster twentieth-century dictator, nor that of a murderous member of the Ku Klux Klan, nor even that of a rabble-rousing politician who knows how to play people one against the other for personal gain. Iago is, rather, the government official, the doctor, the lawyer, the businessman, the architect, the teacher—anyone who is for whatever reasons unsatisfied enough with his or her life (no matter its privileges) to feel relentlessly spiteful—though secretly so. A smart man, a brilliantly manipulative man, an ever-so-shrewdly sly man, he knows how to take the measure of someone else—bring him down by bringing out the worst in him: Othello's self-doubt become his crazy suspicions.

Who of us has never felt moments of Iago's insinuating mean-spiritedness—masked as tactful, advisory generousness? Who of us is immune, as Othello was not, to the unnerving asides of others offered under the guise of helpful suggestion, persuasion, even friendly assistance? *Othello* is tough, demanding theater—relentless in its unblinkered insistence on the soul's darker side as a commonplace aspect of this existence. Shakespeare wants us to attend to that darkness, Iago's, as it infectiously takes hold of Othello, of a whole world, with all sorts of consequences. Long before the paradigms of social science befell us, and well before the first African was forcibly brought to the shores of what would one day become the United States, the great bard knew that appearances can belie emotional reality, that there is, so to speak, darkness and darkness—and that, finally, as Ralph Ellison never stopped reminding us, racism is a selective blindness with respect to our shared rock-bottom humanity. Othello the Moor becomes a victim of that darkness, his own as it is stirred, fueled by, engages with Iago's. *Othello* shines light on a darkness whose lurking presence can be found in all of us, as the Bible keeps insisting, and as my teaching colleague surely knew when he chose to assign a particular play in a course otherwise devoted to twentieth-century issues as they are rendered in fiction and essays.

Bonhoeffer's position in society, his personal safety, and, if need be, his very life were not to be defended at all costs.

This past summer I spent most of my reading hours with the writings of the German theologian, pastor, and ultimately, martyr, Dietrich Bonhoeffer. I had first been introduced to his work, and been told the story of his life, by my teacher Perry Miller, whose research explored the provocative wisdom in the sermons and essays of the New England Puritan divines of the seventeenth and eighteenth centuries. To this day I recall Miller's account of Bonhoeffer's willful stand against the Nazis—a singular, voluntary opposition to tyranny that culminated in his execution in a concentration camp only weeks before the end of Hitler's regime. Miller himself was obviously haunted by Bonhoeffer's life—this Lutheran, this "Aryan" of great social, economic, and educational privilege who refused to embrace the führer and his henchmen, as the great majority of Germany's ministers all too evidently did, many of them even wearing the swastika as they went about their so-called spiritual duties. To this day, also, I recall Miller's challenge to us in his seminar: "What would you do under such circumstances?"

By the time that question had been put to the class, not one of us was able to answer with any moral confidence. A remarkably vigorous and knowing teacher had immersed us in the Germany of the early 1930s, in Bonhoeffer's personal life—his family background, his religious training, his early career as a scholar—and we had thereby come to realize that by no means was the outcome of his life (death at thirty-nine) predictable during many of the years that preceded it, even the late 1930s, when he had made his principled, energetic opposition to the Third Reich quite clear. Bonhoeffer's life, like that of so many idealists, took shape gradually—a growing response to a growing evil whose contours time and events only gradually revealed.

In medical school at Columbia University's College of Physicians and Surgeons, I followed Miller's advice and took a seminar given by Reinhold Niebuhr, a friend of Bonhoeffer's. Twice in the 1930s the young religious intellectual from Berlin had come to Union Theological Seminary to study. Niebuhr was, of course, no stranger to irony, and he was at pains for us to realize how concerned many at Union were for Bonhoeffer when he decided, in 1939, to leave America (after being here only a month or so) for his native land. By then Bonhoeffer's explicit, sustained, risky, brave resistance to the Nazis was thoroughly established. He might have stayed in the United States and helped awaken a still strongly isolationist nation to the great threat fascism posed for the Western democracies. But he wanted to take his stand amid his own people—though in 1939 he emphatically did not have imprisonment and a martyred death on his mind. Some of his friends at Union, however, had his choice of a return to Germany very much on their minds, as Niebuhr let us know loud and clear: "It was tempting for many here to regard him as in trouble psychologically, as depressed. It was tempting to recommend that he see a psychiatrist—then he'd become more 'realistic.'"

Last August, as I read yet again Eberhard Bethge's biography of Bonhoeffer and Bonhoeffer's own words, I realized how shrewd Niebuhr was to remind us of the disparity of thought and assumption between modern psychiatry, and yes, even certain precincts of contemporary religion, with its emphasis on "pastoral counseling," on the one hand, and, on the other, the eventual, reluctant yet unyielding realization on Bonhoeffer's part that his position in society, his personal safety, and, if need be, his very life were not to be defended at all costs, were not to be his bottom line, but were, in a sense, up for grabs. "The cost of discipleship," to use his phrase, the cost, that is, of a loyalty under great duress to Jesus, to his example (his life as he chose to experience it) can be high, indeed—beyond the imagining, really, of some of us who are called "normal" and who surely would have known (in Bonhoeffer's situation) how to be "realistic," as Niebuhr put it so searchingly, bluntly.

"This is the end—but for me the beginning of life"—those last recorded words of Bonhoeffer's remind us how topsy-turvy a Christian life can be, how utterly indifferent to, even contrary to various received secular pieties, not least the psychological ones that offer us "the reality principle" and "normality" as conceptual judgments of our behavior. "Rebuked and scorned," as the phrase goes, Jesus did not play it cool and cagey, did not temper his message or his behavior in order to avoid "conflict" or "anxiety" or "depression," in order to "work on this or that problem." Rather, he pressed on, acting on principles that to others seemed incomprehensible or dangerous, even life-threatening—the essential "madness" of a kind of spiritual determination that won't settle for the rewards of "adjustment." Similarly, while others (many who called themselves Christians and attended church regularly) cannily cut their views and actions to suit the political power of the day, Bonhoeffer threw caution to the winds and realized that, in the poet Paul Celan's words, "death is a master from Germany"—hence the requirement of standing up to it, even if to do so defies all that others deem to be "practical" or a matter of "common sense." No wonder, then, that a young Jesuit who teaches in my undergraduate course recently wished, wistfully, that the Catholic Church would one day make Dietrich Bonhoeffer its "first ecumenical saint"—he who lived as if Jesus were a concrete, nearby presence, constantly insisting that deeds, not clever-spoken or written words, not practiced rituals galore, are the test of a particular faith's significance in one's life.

*Psychotherapy, in all its American banality, is
redeemed through its emphasis on the personal as part
of the communal.*

During the 1970s I spent a lot of time talking with children who lived in South Boston and Cambridge in Massachusetts— so-called "working-class" people trying to make a go of it, no matter the sometimes tough circumstances of their lives. In South Boston, many of the people I met, whose homes I visited, felt left out of things; they saw a city prospering, but themselves getting no share of that affluence. Moreover, they knew that the liberal intellectuals who resided professionally in the abundance of nearby universities had no real interest in them—indeed, regarded them all too unfavorably, labeled them with an assortment of stereotypes. In Cambridge, the families I met felt very much the same way—overlooked, if not patronized or worse, by those who inhabited those same universities, which make that city's reputation so big across the nation and beyond.

The father of one of the children I was getting to know in Cambridge worked for the subway system, known as the MBTA (Massachusetts Bay Transportation Authority). Every day he walked through the Harvard Yard on his way to work. (He "drove" the subway from Harvard Square to the working-class neighborhoods south of the city.) That yard, the heart of a university's life, is open to the public; yet he always felt himself an outsider, a stranger walking on its paths, which offered him a convenient shortcut. He had a sharp eye for the students and teachers he passed, a good ear for what they said and how they said it: "I go through [the Harvard Yard] and I overhear the people—they're really sure of themselves. This is their world, and when they're through the whole world will be theirs. I'm sure a lot of people who go there, they're OK; they're just trying to catch ahold of the ladder and climb up. But there are some who think they are God's gift to humanity—they're full of themselves to overflowing. They're on top or they're on the express train to the top; and, you know, they treat that college as if it's theirs—they were born to go there. It's not 'the Yard'; it's their backyard. They've traveled everywhere—except a few blocks away to where people like me live! They're big shots already, before they're old enough to get a drink legally, and it shows on their faces and in the way they speak."

There was more, much more—a worker and walker who had an eye, an ear for the smugness, the arrogance, the self-importance that he occasionally encountered. I thought of that man as I recently watched *Good Will Hunting* at a neighborhood theater. The action of the movie takes place in Cambridge, where I teach, and South Boston, my old place of work (home visits, volunteer teaching in the elementary public schools). In the movie, a janitor at MIT is also a math wizard—and soon becomes known to a professor, who wants to wrest him from his neighborhood street-life in order that he may join a privileged company of scientific intellectuals.

When the young man refuses to jump at this chance of a lifetime and shows himself to be unimpressed by and even scornful of this opportunity to leave one world and join another, the explanation is obvious: he is in psychological trouble and badly needs help. He is indeed in trouble, but not necessarily for the reasons his "betters" (the professor and his ilk) think. A few absurdly pretentious psychiatrists show why the young man is distrustful of those who patronize him with their admiration for his intellect or their clinical appraisals of his "problems." It is a psychologist, himself rooted firmly in the youth's world (he teaches at a community college and lives in South Boston), who will get to this gifted, skeptical, poignantly wry, observant, and prickly fellow and help him say good-bye to one community and a tentative hello, through a girlfriend, to another.

Echoes of *Jude the Obscure* keep rising in this film, written and acted by Ben Affleck and Matt Damon, two Cambridge youths who themselves have taken the measure of a city's class barriers. They are knowing, morally energetic writers, and they are already most accomplished actors.

With the help of a daring and quirky director (Gus Van Sant) and a similarly quirky Robin Williams, they do a wonderful end run around Hollywood's cautions and stuffiness, its clichés become prohibitions. The film offers powerful populist moments that analyze the greed of imperial capitalism the way the popes did in *Rerum Novarum* and *Quadragesimo Anno*. Vigorous and sly satire mingles suggestively, provocatively with two affecting love stories, that of a young man and his girlfriend and of a patient and his therapist. Jude Fawley's awakened sense of class conflict, his defiant realization of what Christminster (Oxford) is all about, is Will Hunting's similar struggle to avoid a moral surrender to people and places he has every right to question as well as to regard with curiosity and desire.

Psychotherapy, in all its American banality, is redeemed through its emphasis on the personal as part of the communal. How do we learn to hold on to what matters in our experienced life while allowing for new journeys? And how, above all, do we "rise" without falling into a moral swamp (the phoniness and conniving of a kind of "success")? Now, one suspects, these two young and gifted writers and actors will have plenty of cause to test themselves in real life as they have their character do in the movie. They, like him, are "hunting," are well along the chase of achievement, but no doubt are desperately trying to hold on to their "good will" against the corrosions and duplicities of cultural hype as it comes their way in great public abundance.

I wondered if she really believed what she seemed to believe, whether she wasn't really quite frightened "underneath."

During my internship year I spent a month with patients, most of whom were dying of blood diseases, various kinds of leukemia, the lymphomas. At that time, the middle years of this century, we didn't have the powerful chemotherapeutic drugs that now go a long way toward a cure in many instances of such diseases—though, alas, there is much more we need to know, and many still succumb to the kinds of illnesses young doctors like me, back then, could only resist with one blood transfusion after another.

To this day, memories of that hospital experience keep coming to me, especially when I lose perspective about life, get all caught up in some situation that seems to be the most important matter this side of Kingdom Come—only to recall what happened way back then, when I not only was trying to get blood into exceedingly vulnerable and weak patients, but was having conversations with them and, not rarely, learning a lot from them about what truly counts in this life and what is of little consequence.

I remember in particular a young woman of about thirty, the mother of two small girls, who was dying of what we had diagnosed as acute myeloid leukemia. Her husband was an English teacher in a Chicago high school, and I winced when he and the two children would arrive to be with someone all three of them knew was in great jeopardy. Yet the husband seemed strongly composed, even cheerful, and his daughters, just old enough to be in the early years of elementary school, were constantly attentive to their mother, with no evident anxiety or fearfulness. I knew that both my patient and her husband were well aware of her poor prospects, and I also knew that both had taken pains to tell their children what most likely was ahead. The older of the girls announced to me one afternoon while I was at her mom's bedside: "God is deciding when he'll be asking our mother to come visit him." A pause, and then her ominous afterthought: "And it may be soon, you know."

I most certainly did know; and I also "knew," at that time in my life, to be troubled by what I was seeing and hearing—an almost eerie calm and composure in a patient and her family as a mortal illness relentlessly and quite evidently was closing in on them. I was, then, by no means willing to ignore this family's way of behaving. My head was all full of psychiatric thinking: they were resorting to "massive denial"; they were far more anxious and fearful than they could let on, even to one another, let alone me; in the long run they would need "help" in coming to terms with the sadness in their lives, the considerable anger as well—that such a tragedy should have befallen them, out of the blue.

I had no time to dwell on that psychiatric line of thinking; I was overwhelmed with my medical obligations, to the point that I was lucky to get three or four hours sleep on any given night. Early one evening I was called to the bedside of the woman I have just described. She was having trouble breathing; her pulse was unsteady; and, not least, her transfusion was in trouble and needed to be fixed (or started again in another vein).

After I examined her, got the blood going and figured out that she was in no acute or immediate peril, I paused to ask her how her family was doing. She told me that they were all right, that she did "sometimes" worry about them, but she had great confidence in their ability to manage without her. I was surprised by what she said—the first time she had, by implication, acknowledged the gravity of things, the future that awaited her husband and two youngsters.

But now she changed the subject; she asked me how I was doing. I quickly said "OK." She smiled and begged to differ: "I knew you'd say that, but I know it's not true." I was surprised, then more than a little confused and, finally, irritated. In no time I had mobilized a host of psychiatric and psychoanalytic words to take care of her, so to speak—she wasn't really able to accept her own bleak prospects, so she was ascribing to me worries really felt about herself, her kin. I kept such thoughts to myself, of course—merely insisted upon my "OK" condition—whereupon she told me this: "I see you here on the ward day and night, and I see how tired you are. I include you in my prayers." She went on to thank me for the "help" I'd offered her in the last few weeks of her hospitalization, and she told me, further, that she would keep praying for me, "from wherever God decides to put me."

I hadn't the slightest idea what to say in response, other than a polite expression of thanks. Later, I wondered if she really believed what she seemed to believe, whether she wasn't really quite frightened "underneath" (where all truth lies!), whether she really didn't need to talk with one of our hospital psychiatrists, who might help her discuss what I had no time to hear. Soon enough she would be dying, and doing so in apparent calm, even with a touch of humor, which she shared with us on the hospital staff as well as her family. And to this day I think of her and wonder whether, when my time to leave this life here comes, I'll have even a small measure of her quiet faith—not only in God's scheme of things, but also in others around her, and in herself, too.

I could lecture on the moral and social inquiry and
myself behave like a moral and social outcast.

I worked hard some time ago on a lecture that meant a lot to me—about
Raymond Carver's short fiction, his poetry and his personal writing
(essays about his life and his reading preferences). I use his stories all
the time, especially "Cathedral" and "A Small, Good Thing," both in the
collection titled *Where I'm Calling From*, which was published posthu-
mously (he died in 1988 at the age of fifty). For years I taught Carver in
conjunction with Edward Hopper's paintings and prints, which I showed
the students as slides. Carver's world is mostly made up of working-class
people, men and women struggling hard to stay afloat against considerable
odds, be they some aspect of our social and economic system or of their
own psychological life. Sometimes these late twentieth-century Americans
are down, but not out; they have glimpsed a redemptive possibility here
and there, no matter the melancholy tug of their lives—though in some
instances, alas, an unrelieved bleakness stares the reader in the face. So
with Hopper's visual scenes: they give expression at times to a qualified
expectancy, if not hope; but, not rarely, they, too, candidly remind us
how lost we can be—sadly out of sorts and withdrawn from others, or
confused about our purpose in this heavily commercial, impersonal, urban

life of office buildings and apartment houses and subways and cafeterias and coffee shops.

During the lecture I read from the stories of this American master, a direct, accomplished descendant of Chekhov. I read from his sometimes heart-breaking, sometimes humorous, always quite humble poems. I read from his autobiographical writing. I showed slides of Hopper's work. I tried to make connections between those two enormously talented Americans, even as I offered interpretations of and discursive commentary on a writer's fiction, an artist's pictures. I worked hard to get at the moral implications of what we were studying—the way, for example, Carver confronts us with our own blindness as he tells us what a blind man enabled his sighted host to "see." Hopper's paintings, though relatively well known, often prompt a noticeable stiffness in the students—as if they have been compelled to see an intended warning: Look out, there is danger aplenty ahead, lots of mixed signals, no small amount of the "alienation" that philosophers have discussed in recent times.

By the end of the lecture I hoped to have relayed some information, conveyed the spirit of two gifted observers of this country's life, sparked enough interest in the students so that they would explore, become familiar with "Carver country," as his writing has been called, and also with Hopper's unnerving, brooding takes on the way we live now. I was hoping for a responsive passion in the students—that they would really connect with Carver, comprehend what it is that Hopper wants them to know. After I had finished, I thought I'd accomplished my purpose—a host of students were anxious to ask questions, seek references, share their own stories. I left the lecture hall with a sense of reasonable satisfaction—an important lecture, so I saw it, reasonably well delivered. I felt that with the help of an exceptionally knowing writer and a visionary artist I had been able to discuss that most important moral matter—how one lives a life, to what purpose.

Soon enough I was on my way home. I had errands to do, an afternoon appointment to keep. I had, as mentioned, been delayed by conversation with students at the end of the lecture—young people who wanted to have serious reflective exchanges. Now I started making up for my late departure from Cambridge. As a light turned yellow, telling me to slow down, stop, I accelerated, went through it as it showed red. As a car progressed through a city street all too slowly for my taste, I quickly passed it, not the right thing to do on a two-lane thoroughfare. Once at the highway I started maneuvering, going faster than the posted speed limit, zooming in and out of lanes, while all the time keeping my eye out for the police. Eventually, I saw a state police car parked on the side of the road—a speeder had been stopped, was being ticketed—so the odds were now high I'd be spared. I plunged onward, glancing at the car's clock, at the rear view mirror, and, of course, at the road ahead, each lane an invitation, each car an obstacle, each minute a challenge to cover more distance. I was doing fine, no matter the array of lights popping on behind me—worried, irate individuals, righteously signaling their discontent with and disapproval of a fast-traveling driver.

At last the downward slope toward my hometown. I am arrogantly, thoughtlessly pleased with myself—a ten-mile stretch covered in near record time. Suddenly I see police cars everywhere, four or five of them, their lights flashing—ahead of me, though—and in their midst two cars badly damaged: a serious accident. I am a physician. I stop my car. I go to ask if I can be of help. But an ambulance arrives almost as I speak, and the three injured people are taken away.

I stand there thinking. I consider the huge irony—that I could lecture with apparent success on the moral and social inquiry enabled by, stirred by writers and artists—and myself behave like a moral and social outcast. It is hard, it seems, for some of us to live up to what we so readily urge upon others. At home—late, late, late—I wondered how long I would remember that lesson in such a way that it might give some shape to my lived life.

Once more I took note of the psychological acuity, the capacity to figure out others with a certain thoughtful detachment.

During the 1970s, at the height of a racial conflict in Boston prompted by a federal court order that African American students be admitted to schools across the city in the interest of a better education, I got to know a number of those youths—high schoolers who lived in Roxbury and were bused to South Boston, a mostly Irish Catholic neighborhood. In no time people were at one another's throats.

Those who lived in Roxbury were anxious to break out of poverty and the long-enforced isolation as well that had been the fate of their ancestors—slavery, then segregation down South, and finally, up North, neighborhood schools commonly overcrowded, understaffed, educationally inadequate. Those who lived in South Boston, so-called "working-class families," regarded themselves as victims. "Their" school was now under the control of a judge who himself lived outside of the city. And that was the bottom (residential) line: If you had money, you could buy your way out of the uncertainty and tumult of a court-supervised social and racial crisis. Indeed, if you had money, you could live in some of Boston's swankier neighborhoods and send your children to private schools.

At the time, though, the "class" side of the issue was buried under the outburst of anger, on both sides, connected to "race"—and, of course, it was not lost on many in either Roxbury or South Boston that many of those most in favor of this version of "integration" were white people who lived outside Boston, untouched by the strains of such a struggle.

I was going to that high school, talking with young men and women coming there by bus from Roxbury and with those who had always come there from the streets of South Boston. I had studied school desegregation in the South, and now I was observing it in the city where I'd been born and grew up. One African American student I got to know, Mary Ann, was a remarkably stoic and farsighted person who kept telling me she "understood" the evident anger of some of the white people of the city. "It's new, and they're scared," she said tersely.

As I listened to her I often wondered whether I would be able, under such circumstances, to summon for myself that kind of understanding—to put myself in the shoes of others who weren't being welcoming to me. I chalked up some of Mary Ann's generosity of spirit to her good-natured, hopeful temperament. She was a cheerful, bright young lady, and she was determined, as well, to outlast the cold, unfriendly reception she was receiving all the time.

But four months into that experience, Mary Ann's grandmother suddenly died of a stroke, and the girl was devastated. The grandmother had effectively been Mary Ann's mom, because her mother worked hard and long cleaning rooms in a Boston hotel and had to contend, as well, with rheumatoid arthritis. The grandmother's sudden death, at only fifty-eight, stunned everyone in her family—and Mary Ann was more than tempted to leave school, get a job, and try to take care of her ailing, hard-pressed mother and her younger siblings. Yet she stayed on, though obviously saddened. She had usually worn bright clothes; now she dressed in black. She had usually tried to smile, answer questions eagerly and spiritedly in class; now she was slow to respond, distracted. She should be in that "fancy hotel cleaning up after those rich folks," she told me once.

One day, when I came to talk with Mary Ann, she had an "incident" to report: "A girl came up to me in the hall. They never talk to me, so I was surprised. She asked if I was 'all right.' I said yes, sure. She said she noticed I was wearing black all the time. I said yes, my gramma died. She said she was sorry. Then she told me her father died a year ago, and she knew what I was going through. It was nice of her." Nicer still that the girl, Alice, dared break with her many South Boston school friends and kept talking with Mary Ann—not the kind of behavior likely to earn her applause from her friends.

Alice asked Mary Ann if there was anything she could do to be of help. No, there wasn't. Finally, Alice asked for Mary Ann's address so she could send a "sympathy card." Mary Ann was touched but skeptical: "She's still upset because of her father, that's why she's trying to be nice to me."

Once more I took note of the psychological acuity, the capacity to figure out others with a certain thoughtful detachment. But a month or so later, Mary Ann found herself less readily comprehending, puzzled by what she heard. Alice told her that she was sorry for all that had been happening there at South Boston High School and told her she personally regretted her outspoken disapproval of earlier days. Then, this from Mary Ann: "She told me she owes us [the African American students] an 'act of contrition,' and I didn't know what she was talking about. I was confused. So I asked her, and she said the priest told her, if you do something, and you figure out it's wrong, then you should recognize that you've made your error and try to make up for it some way. You face up to what you've done and pray you won't do it again. I think that's why she sent the [sympathy] card to us, as 'an act of contrition.'"

I didn't know what to say—so I joked and said I'd learned a new word, *contrition*! I told her, "I'd never have heard of that word if I hadn't come here to this school!"

*This child knew that misdeeds deserve, warrant an
expression of regret.*

In a recent column I mentioned "contrition," a word heard a few years
ago for the first time by an African American girl of Protestant faith who
had been bused to a school whose students were mostly of Catholic (and
Irish) background. The black child was puzzled by the word, only to learn
from one of her white classmates that the heart of contrition had to do with
"regret." For the white student contrition was familiar—"something priests
say when they want you to apologize and admit you've made a mistake."
For the black child contrition conveyed a certain elusive mystery: "I think
it means you've done something that can get you in trouble, but whether
you meant to do the wrong thing, that's up to God to decide, so you can't
be sure, and he's the one who is watching, and he knows."

I was intrigued and stirred mightily when I heard that remark, which
struck me as powerfully suggestive in its implications—the notion that
God is a moral companion of sorts to us, that he observes us and comes
to conclusions about our episodes of wrongdoing, no matter our claims,
excuses, self-justifications. A heavy weight, I recall thinking in my psychoanalytic and psychiatric mode—the very idea that we can err, and that
our missteps are noticed and go on record.

In contrast, the word "guilty" predominates for many of us today, but with a subjective emphasis. The black child put her finger on me and my kind when she favored me with an ironic gesture: "You see, if you go and do a bad thing, your conscience will make you sweat and you'll feel down in the dumps, my granny says, so you'd better behave, or you'll lose your appetite and you'll toss and turn right through the night. But Granny says it's more important what you do than whether you're upset because of what you did. She says we should go check in with our minister, and let him tell us the right and the wrong, whether we're on God's side, or we've gone and strayed!"

There it all is, and here we are—on many talk shows and sometimes in churches, in an occasional school and in certain homes: guilt as a "problem," something to be addressed through a conversation that aims at awareness, if not (Lord, save us) "insight." Interestingly, at that Boston school, a convergence had occurred. The black child had heard from her white age-mate and classmate echoes of her own religious and family background. She had heard thoughts about regret and remorse, about sadness as a felt response to deeds acknowledged and recognized as thoroughly bad, as malevolent in nature: the heckling of newcomers through resort to racial epithets or scornful personal comments. A priest had intervened, called such words worthy of contrition, and several black children who were the targets of such language had, in turn, worried whether their hostile critics might be soon enough feeling "guilty."

Those critics, too, struggled with that word, and with another one, too, as a Catholic child told me: "I should have kept quiet. I think the priest wants us to be nicer to them [the African American children at school with her], but I'm not sure what he thinks we should do. Maybe he thinks we should be sorry. That's what contrition is, to be sorry. I asked the priest: 'Should I feel bad, and take my sister's advice? She says, "You either go on a guilt trip or you don't."' The priest said, 'No, you go visit God; you go that way and you'll know.' But my sister says you should get guilt off your back. The priest says God gave us backs to carry things. He said, 'If you've gone down the wrong road, you need God to get the right road directions.' My sister says, 'It's you you should help—get your head cleared, so you're not overloaded with guilt.'" I asked her whose advice she preferred. She responded, "I think I should vote for the priest!"

Her explanation, her story, rang in my ears—a jolt almost: that when we err, we ought to feel regret, sadness, remorse (as opposed to talking and talking about our "guilt"). I also kept remembering a moment's unself-conscious act by that white girl—she lowered her head briefly, as she spoke, and then raised it, her eyes still looking at me, her mouth closed. She seemed strangely at peace with herself and in no need of speaking—her sister's pressing, ever so contemporary psychological advice notwithstanding.

Later, as I tried to understand what had happened to this girl, how her mind had worked, I began to realize that her head had, in fact, spoken to me. This child knew that misdeeds deserve, warrant an expression of regret, and she was willing to embrace melancholy unashamedly and, as well, affirm a willingness to make public her awareness (her earnest and fervent hope) that the Lord who sees mistakes made will also see something quite real and important: contrition expressed and conveyed through a head's movement, through eyes widened in silent, knowing penitence.

Our insistent yearnings ought not to be the stuff of glib psychiatric pronouncements.

We have been told lately, in the name of religion, that homosexuals are sinners, and that if they only accepted that notion, they would be entitled to a new moral and theological status. They would be among the saved, which means, presumably, those who have acknowledged their wrongdoing and thereby returned to the Lord's fold. What are the rest of us to make of this new outburst of spiritual accusation directed at thousands, even millions, whose desires of heart and mind have been turned into a matter of errant choice, if not outright evil in the biblical sense? What are we to make of these claims to be able to "cure" homosexual people?

When Freud, the first psychoanalyst, was asked by the mother of a homosexual man what was proper for her to feel and think about her son and what his clinical prospects might be, the great explorer of the human mind, of our passions and preferences (who at the time was much criticized by various religious leaders) responded with humility and compassion—humility by making no claim to be able to reverse out of hand what he knew to be a complex life already substantially set in its ways;

compassion out of a doctor's quiet decency and a scientist's interest in understanding and responding to another human being.

Who can say how such an attitude on the part of a brilliant psychological healer would be regarded today by those who claim to know so much about this aspect of our human feeling, an aspect so much a part of many lives, as those of us who work in schools and colleges, in clinics of various kinds, well know? Like others of my profession, I have "worked with" men and women who came to see me out of anxiety and worry; and I have tried hard to learn from them about their lives, dreams, and attachments, their interests and preoccupations.

Again and again I hear the word "homosexual" used or various kinds of heterosexuality mentioned with acceptance or regret, fearful panic or apprehension and, not rarely, with the same alarmed curiosity that prompts so many individuals these days to visit a psychiatrist or psychoanalyst to ask, "How did I become this person I know in my heart I've become (in thought, in desire, in deed), and what might I do to make myself quite another kind of person?"

To be sure, few in our time would doubt that self-reflection and self-knowledge, helped by an informed, experienced, and conscientious psychological clinician, are often remarkably valuable instruments of personal change. Those who once felt "driven," relentlessly drawn to ideas and actions they themselves criticized or condemned, can begin to note that their attitudes have become somewhat different and their feelings quite otherwise in the range and direction of desire. Still, as with any of us, what we find interesting and attractive tells a lot about how we have been brought up, who our parents were, what we learned from them and about them. Hence the power of our particular interests in other people.

This is all now unsurprising and part of received knowledge. Yet Freud knew well that human complexity and ambiguity, our moral makeup and insistent yearnings toward certain other persons, ought not to be the stuff of quick psychological conclusions and glib psychiatric pronouncements. Much less should it be subject to the denunciatory and exclusionary excesses of those who are ready to rid themselves of others in a body politic. He went so far (an indication of his generous, unafraid humanism, putting many of us in the same basket, as it were) that he even spoke of homosexual feeling as a passing part of most everyone's psychological development. We have mothers and fathers; we are daughters or sons, and, of course, we grow up intimately connected to people of the same sex. Hence the numerous "variations on a theme," as the expression goes: the manner in which we come to feel stirred or scared with regard to sex or to one or another kind of person.

To fly in the face of such clinical awareness, of generations of stories told in offices to psychologists, psychiatrists, and psychoanalysts, who want to attend to and learn from their patients, is to retreat sadly and with an obvious, eager insistence from what is now clinically informed rationality. What Freud long ago knew, we are entitled to know. How ironic, then, that today our homosexuals are called "sinners" and are told to repent, even as Freud's ideas were repeatedly called "sinful," early in his career by his Austrian accusers, and by others elsewhere as his ideas spread across national borders.

One wonders, of course, whether this new embrace of will in the name of God (homosexuality as a sin, reversible through appeal to prayer and in response to an intense, spiritually connected criticism) will work among gay men and women, any more than that approach has worked among heterosexuals, including even prominent clergymen, who have not shown themselves capable of successfully willing a change in their sensual interests under the assault of reproach or self-reproach in the name of the Bible.

One wonders, too, whether those who have chosen to castigate others for such religious reasons will stop short at the sexual and find their consciences satisfied. Or will they, for instance, go on to remember the parable of the camel and its difficulty getting through the eye of a needle, as that tale was used about the rich and their eventual entrance to heaven? Will we then have aroused, finger-pointing picketing on Wall Street, with our bankers and investors there denounced as sinners, and with their consuming habits declared reversible through prayer?

*These youngsters recognize that smart or powerful is
not necessarily the same as good.*

L
ike so many in our nation, I have found President Clinton's personal difficulties, not to mention the intense public scrutiny of
them, all too unsettling. I spend my time with the young. From
time to time, when I can get away from my college responsibilities, I teach
in an elementary school and a high school. I have been troubled by what
I've heard from those youngsters of varying backgrounds. They, like the
rest of us, have kept trying to make sense of this important leader of ours,
a lawyer from an important law school and winner of an important award
that took him to an important university across the Atlantic. Here is what
I heard from a seventh-grade class in a junior high, all the youths about
twelve years old, on the brink of adolescence. I was trying to teach "current
events," and was having no difficulty getting a class to talk about our
country's present-day news. A usually perceptive youth who is normally
quiet now talked and talked, a voluble response on his part to what he
heard at home and in the neighborhood.

"I can't believe this guy Clinton, this president," the lad declared amid
laughs and murmurs. After encouragement by me to speak his mind (I
had a tape recorder going), he offered a blunt, moral skepticism. "How

can a guy who's got as far as he has, way to the top, be so dumb? He's won the country, and he's made a dope of himself. He may lose his job any day. He can't control himself. All those brains and he ruins himself! It goes to show you, just because you get way up there you can get totally lost, so you go down the drain, and everyone's watching."

In reply, a girl sitting two seats in front of this speaker speaks her mind: "He is just a wise guy—you can see it on his face. He smirks, and he thinks people don't catch on. I feel sorry for his daughter, she seems nice. I wonder what she's thinking—what she'd say if she was right here, with us? He's a type, you know, the president, the kind of guy who hasn't learned to grow up, to control himself—fooling everyone, but he fools himself, that's what, and so it's a big price he's paying."

I hear more and more young Americans in their own thoughtful, provocative manner unpretentiously mixing moral and psychological analysis as they approach one riddle after another. I hear those youngsters say that smart or powerful is not necessarily the equivalent of good, that age and authority don't always go with good judgment or self-control, and, not least, that adulation of a big shot can be dangerous. Hence the need, as one student put it, to "watch out if you start putting all your dough in some dude's basket, and he goes and runs away, and you're left with nothing." After which he adds, "So you should go find some place to pray, and there you don't bow before a politician who's full of himself."

As I listen I feel sad for all of us in the room, for our country. I am annoyed later, as the boys mock the president with sexual language, mock his impulsivity and its satisfactions with tough street talk, and as the girls laugh at Monica Lewinsky, make fun of her office liaison and, indeed, summon a cynical, sexual language with respect to her pleasures and purposes. These crudities are in the minds of millions of us across this land—jokes and more jokes as we try to comprehend a big story featured day after day in print and on videotape.

"What do you think?" I was eventually asked by members of my class and fellow teachers in that school. I tried to be tactful and protested my ignorance of the parties involved, even as I was asked about them, their psychological nature, their mental life. I told the class, finally, that I agreed with some of what I'd heard them say, in class and out of it. I tried to expand upon "psychology," on the way our passions overcome our common sense, our better judgment. I was, in fact, lecturing in what I hoped was a vernacular that was not academic or off-putting. I was trying to nod to their intuitions while declaring my moral feelings, my awareness of life's complex and ironic events. I told them of anonymous stories I'd heard in my hospital office long ago, of men who were unhappy at home and who became involved with women at work, and of women who felt they needed to use their bodies to gain success at work, or self-respect.

None of that, in this age of Oprah, is surprising to any of us, nor was it surprising to those about-to-be teenagers. Yet as I heard myself speak, I realized how helpful it was for me—as I had hoped our class discussions would be for the children—to put the matter in a shared, everyday perspective. Yes, we can try to make psychiatric generalizations about adulterous older men, about seductive or vulnerable young women. But as those boys and girls had reminded me, comparable lessons are all around us for consideration. And there is, finally, the melancholy pity of it all: the moral tale that eludes a factuality endlessly pursued, even furtively so, by a grim, tight-lipped investigator who must be stirring Nathaniel Hawthorne to imaginative fancy, wherever he resides in eternity's scheme of things.

"I wished he'd been as understanding and kindly at home with his family as he was in the world with all his associates."

In the early 1970s, at a meeting attended by a host of psychiatrists and psychoanalysts, Erik H. Erikson (then at work on Gandhi's life and on political activity as it is engaged, sometimes, with minds, even souls) spoke to us, eagerly assembled, about his intellectual struggle to make sense of a great leader. (The book was eventually published as *Gandhi's Truth*.) He also spoke about his "troubles" with a particular individual much admired throughout the world. Erikson was a child psychoanalyst, trained by Anna Freud, who in Vienna during the 1920s initiated applications of her father's thinking to therapeutic work with children. "When I learned about Gandhi," Erikson told us, "I kept wondering about his wife and children—and I have to admit, I worried about them."

I was listening with a tape recorder at hand, because I was working on a biographical study of Erikson. I helped teach in a course he gave at Harvard College, joined his seminars, and heard him speak to audiences whenever I could. That time he was especially candid and poignant as he shared his concerns, provoked by a writing project. "I had to have something out with him [Gandhi]," he told us, and then this: "I sat there in a daze, unable to put on paper what was crossing my mind—until, I felt the need, the desire, to write this man a letter. He was dead, but he was certainly alive in my mind, and finally, there I was writing a letter to him—I told him (to be brief) that I wished he'd been as understanding and kindly at home with his family as he was in the world with all his associates and followers, and yes, with his enemies, the ones he was confronting and opposing."

I can still see, with those words spoken, Erikson's head lowered, even a momentary shake of the head—irony and ambiguity as almost heart-stopping in their capacity to give us much reflective pause. Erikson did, however, proceed; he spoke of Gandhi's spiritual and political triumphs, no matter his not altogether happy personal life as a family man—and of course, many of us in that room weren't totally surprised, because we'd seen such a disparity in many of our apparently successful young or older patients: smashing achievement in schools or college or in the worlds of law, business, medicine—yet, all the while, a failure to measure up humanly and therefore morally to the accomplishments being accumulated in classes or workplaces.

Years later, the novelist Walker Percy would summarize what we were discussing at that meeting when he described a character of his in *The Second Coming* as one of those people who get all A's and flunk ordinary living. And I recall well Erik Erikson trying to say as much—though not as pointedly, and not with such a catching punch—when he mused: "It can happen that the qualities that make for good in one part of someone's life don't necessarily have the same effect on that person's 'other life,' you can call it." He became suggestive then—made mention of the "secret side of many brilliant people," or the "cost" of such accomplishments to others, those forsaken or ignored, even insulted or injured—a melancholy matter for all of us to ponder.

Still, our lecturer wanted to move us in another direction, stir us as he'd been stirred while he got to "know" Gandhi, as it were, through reading him, taking in his letters and essays, his remembered remarks. And so for a half-hour or more we heard about "grace," its workings and expression in a life as it connected to other lives. A remarkable spell descended on us, I recall feeling, as that presentation took place, and after it, our responsive discussion. Unfortunately, however, the word "grace," as Erikson eagerly and relaxedly used it, caused evident perplexity in certain of his listeners, who began to move in their chairs, even whisper to one another.

Finally, when the talk was over and we were all given the chance to raise our hands and address the speaker with questions or comments, a prominent psychoanalyst asked "what grace means," and then others, following the lead, posed further questions. They wanted to know the "source" of grace, its "origins in child development," no less. I could see Erikson flushing, moving his right hand through his ample white hair, telltale signs, in him, of agitation, irritation, if not annoyance.

At last he indicated that he was ready to reply, to have his say—but silence reigned while he noted more hands, took more questions, listened to off-the-cuff remarks, each of them aimed at explaining grace through resort to psychoanalytic conceptualization. Upon a last inquiring insistence ("How would you define grace?"), the man sitting in a chair on a slightly raised platform in a hospital conference room looked into the distance of a window and, beyond it, toward the outside sky—and then, these words: "Look, if you have to ask, I'm afraid you'll never know." There we all were, and there our meeting ended—a hurried rush for the door, and surely, inevitably, later, the tic-like buzz of psychological reductionism (what is his problem that caused his evident anger?). But on his way out of that hospital, headed home in a car, Erikson was glad for that moment: "You have to feel sorry for people who won't let anything or anyone be, who have to explain, explain, explain. But that's life, I'm afraid, for many of us who have stumbled into this profession of ours, and maybe I should have been more resigned (or amused!) back there, though there are times when enough is enough!"

A moral leadership that is to work must mobilize a
following in the name of a virtue; it must both inspire
and coerce.

That obedience has to contend with instinct, Terrence Malick's latest movie, *The Thin Red Line*, makes abundantly clear. It is the central psychological exploration in the film. American Marines are in far-off Guadalcanal Island to win a decisive battle with Japanese foes, who have established themselves in a commanding position. Below them are the jungle's wilds and the desirous newcomers, whose landing we behold, and who will have to risk death in order to uphold and complete their mission. The crocodile that figures at the start and the end of the film is meant to make a point about war and conquest, about human nature, and, indirectly, about leadership and its sometimes driving, demanding, relentless affirmation, whether it is pursued up a river in Africa (as in Conrad's *Heart of Darkness*) or in the far Pacific near Australia. But leaders, by definition, have to come to terms with followers, and so those who affirm an intention have to obtain the consent of those whose deeds (their very lives sometimes in jeopardy) are to make the ideal real. This is an utter necessity if the dreams of planners are to be realized. (In the military, they are admirals, generals; in the business world, company officers or, lower down, entrepreneurial bosses such as Conrad chose to give us in his tale of greed come to naught.)

Malick wants to consider the risks attendant upon desire or greed as they get worked into a particular course of action. In this case the action is military—with all the human consequences of moral leadership implemented in a particular setting—namely, a battle for height. Those with the height of leaders who claim a military vision that is being implemented for the sake of a nation's survival and strength ask others to fight for a height—so that the loftiness of a country, and of a fighting tradition (that of the Marine Corps) may be affirmed yet again, secured inch by inch on a selected, then directed, battlefield exertion. An ideal becomes an ordeal. Men die, and their buddies, friends hitherto at their side, must persist or risk the wrath of leaders quick to garb themselves in purpose, rules, mandates, urgencies, customs—the moral paraphernalia of wartime.

Unerringly, fiercely, and implacably, as befits a military story, a movie director gives us a psychoanalytic scenario worthy of Freud's metapsychological theory-making: Eros and Thanatos live "naturally" on an island, but also in the contrived or man-made or artificial ways of military engagement—even as the id of instinct and impulse, of yearning, of affection, of camaraderie with its attachments and bonds, has to meet the superego's agreeable or nay-saying scrutiny (conscience alarmed or persuaded in the name of pieties), and also meet the muster of the ego's watchfulness, its ever-present capability of critical examination, of assessing odds and determining this or that likelihood. A moral leadership that is to work must mobilize a following in the name of a virtue, a cause, an occasion. It must both inspire and coerce others, those two lines of command working together intimately. Malick reminds us that endangered warriors are tied together by affection (the id); but they also harbor the fear and grief, and ultimately the anger, that accompany us when death threatens, takes away those we know, have grown to love and now lose. Our Marines figure out a way to win (the ego's resiliency, canniness); our Marines are loyal (the superego) to their patron military tradition, to their country, and that being the case, they take orders, stick their necks out, stare vividly apparent, noisy, almost certain death in the face.

The Thin Red Line tells of moral leadership that ultimately won't give ground (officers have to shout, make clear their steady conviction, no matter what) and tells also of obedience or compliance or assent—what follows when what is proclaimed, ordered, gets taken to heart, gets believed, even when the clatter of a machine gun threatens not only bodies but the willing minds of followers that are essential for a victory. True, the jungle's law opens and closes the movie—the alligator's appetite; but military law, the ethical constraints of leadership as it gets passed down the ranks, also pervades the film. It is, in fact, its central subject of investigation. Fighting men, who must take orders, must contend with "mourning and melancholia," Freud's phrase become omnipresent. That psychoanalytic abstraction has to do with the fragility of human connection, and when such a vulnerability becomes thoroughly apparent, when ties are sundered, then moral leadership is threatened by hearts broken, by ears become deaf, by eyes looking for a way out rather than the way ahead (up the hill, up to physical conquest, but also to the satisfactions of victory whereby danger has been overcome, survival secured, despite the uneasiness of death felt and lives remembered).

We are left at the film's end with the crocodile's always-unappeased hunger, an aspect not of war but of the earth's everyday animal life—and thereby nudged to think of ourselves, the struggles we wage, hoping to prevail and heeding all along those voices within and about us that urge us to move ahead, notwithstanding the tricky or precarious terrain. Terrence Malick has always known how to render the mind's life sensitively and with great subtlety; now he shows us how a leader connects with followers in a range of ways, with various degrees of intensity, with shifts and shows of emotion that may not be explicit, but clearly come across (are felt, recognized) as defining in their intention, their expectation. The result for us moviegoers is a military and moral narrative that does telling justice to the way we live inside our heads both during war and in peacetime.

Many of us who took to Holden Caulfield, embracing his laid-back words, his wisecracks, his cool, also worried about him. Would he make it?

During the middle years of this fast-waning century J. D. Salinger's *The Catcher in the Rye* became a kind of biblical guide for many young members of the bourgeoisie in the United States. The novel's protagonist, Holden Caulfield, had much going for him—a comfortable suburban life and a privileged educational background in a private school. Yet he seemed ironically vulnerable, for all his sharp intelligence and affluent background. Much of the time he is sardonic, if not cynical, as he takes the measure of teachers and other adults—their inadequacies, their self-importance and smugness, if not arrogance, as those qualities come across in gestures, remarks, and overall manner. Salinger is, of course, walking the familiar path of many a writing storyteller. He spots human frailty and duplicity; he chronicles events; he observes scenes; he tells of the ambiguities, the complexities of a particular world, wherein "phonies" appear to abound. That word is a favorite of Holden's, and one that his creator has him throwing in the face of almost everybody in sight and, by more than implication, at a broad segment of the world's richest, strongest nation.

Needless to say, many of us who took to Holden, embracing his laid-back words, his wisecracks, his cool, it might be called, his mix of wry comment and clever asides meant to put people in their proper places, also worried about him. Would he make it through his bouts of not-so-disguised melancholy, his anger turned into relentlessly unforgiving social scorn, his intense self-absorption having become the reason for a constant isolation and loneliness (the pose of the unyielding outsider a feigned expression of an urgent need for attention)? Still, he saw so much, had evident and contagious humor available to him, and so, we mostly concluded, he would prevail. And so doing he would leave the rest of us clear-headed, as a consequence of his brave jousts with powerful hypocrisy and his mental unmasking of pretense. What he dared see (see through) we could consider our own property. Hence our own consequent clean candor. All the shady deals, all the fake arrangements and agreements, all the deceptions ignored in the name of the conventional, the regular and, alas (speaking of psychiatry as a compliant servant of both), the so-called "normal," had been put squarely on the table by him, enabling an in-your-face attitude on our part, courtesy of a novel's authority and general acceptance, at no cost to us, the eager readers.

Not that Holden was known to everyone, everywhere in his country, as I would eventually discover in the 1960s and beyond, when I got to meet youths who had never heard of him or met him, and some who had passed him by all too readily, even eagerly and angrily, in the course of their high school reading. "This dude, he be sweet on himself, but he turns sour on everyone else!" So I was told by an African American young man who had initiated desegregation in a school full of white and well-to-do students often quite willing to proclaim their affinity to Holden (or his kin, Franny and Zooey, whose names headed other Salinger sagas). The aforementioned loner by virtue of race, amid an ocean of enthusiasts for *The Catcher in the Rye*, went on: "They all caught up in themselves—they think there's nothing they don't know about anyone their eyes fall on, just like their buddy, H.C. I call him." I was so busy then, catching (if I may!) the echo of "caught" with respect to the novel's title, that I failed to take seriously or respectfully that tough psychological appraisal pointedly put forward.

No wonder, years later, in New Haven, as I talked with Anna Freud, hearing her speak of the "young people" she'd met "in the States" as well as England, that African American high schooler came to my mind. "I'm puzzled by the unqualified enthusiasm of so many young people I meet for their age-mate in the story, *The Catcher in the Rye*," Ms. Freud remarked. A pause (while I noted her distinctive, even idiosyncratic way of putting things), and then this: "For many of these high school students, this Mr. Caulfield is a saint—when, in fact, from my reading I gather he is more than frank to admit being a sinner! He never misses an opportunity to let us know how distrustful he is of people, suspicious of them. He is charming, engaging—he is 'honest,' I'm told over and over. 'What do you think, Miss Freud?'—I've been asked a hundred times! I don't think I'll ever answer [that question] as openly and fully as I'd like! I fear I'd fall in the estimation of Holden's fans, if I made mention of his impudence, his freshness (is that why he is so 'refreshing,' I keep wondering when I hear that word?) and very important, his egotism. This is one who turns on others, but has no doubts about himself-—only surliness and smugness when that self-doubt threatens."

Soon enough we were on to a long theoretical discussion of narcissism, a psychoanalytic inquiry of sorts, made by a master clinician and thinker. I regret to say that I had trouble, at least for a while, following the ideas. I was reeling, maybe, with Holden—the both of us brought up short by an ever-incisive clinician who appeared never to miss a trick (in this case, the tricks of an author who had gotten so much of a commitment from us, his readers).

William Carlos Williams treated many Catholics who said they would pray for him. He was skeptical about such promises.

A great privilege it was for me as an undergraduate, then a medical school student, to get to know the New Jersey poet and physician William Carlos Williams. I had written an essay about his long poem *Paterson,* a lyrical evocation of life as it was lived daily and variously in that city where America's first factory was built and, arguably, where our capitalism was born; and my college professor, Perry Miller, urged me to send my effort to the one whose writing had been discussed in all those laboriously typed pages. To my surprise, an envelope came back with a note scribbled on a prescription paper. It was vintage Williams: "Not bad—if you're ever hereabouts, drop by."

It took me time to get up the courage to do so, but I did "drop by." I called the telephone number on the note sent me. I reached Flossie, Williams's wife, and in time I met both of them, got to visit them again and again—a huge jolt to my mind and heart. I remember a discussion with the poet about his Paterson patients, their hopes and worries. He gave a lot of himself to those patients, and often was paid little or nothing for the many house calls he made, over and over, to them, mostly in aging tenement buildings.

Many of the people he treated were Catholics, and often they thanked him for being so attentive, told him they would pray for him. He was, however, explicitly skeptical about such promises, such reported efforts, at home and in church: "I probably should politely say thank you when someone tells me they're praying a lot for me, but I'll be cranky sometimes, because I'm tired (up all night with an emergency!) and besides, I think the good Lord they're addressing, coming at him with their requests—I think he has more needy people to look after; and I don't believe it works that way, that God up there hears all those pleas and answers them, and then goes and does what he's been asked to do! So, I tell people what I think."

He saw a look of surprise come across my face—maybe incredulity with respect to his incredulity. I was silent, and in a moment or two he surprised me further by what he said: "I've had great talks with some of my patients when I tell them what I just told you—we get into religion, of course, even theology! They let me know in their own gentle and respect-ful way that they think I'm naive, never mind walking down the wrong road! 'Of course, God is sitting up there with some long-distance phone, taking messages from us, and giving orders to others'—a grandmother who has only been here [in the United States] ten years or so told me last year; and I could see she was praying hard for me then and there as she spoke. She finished me off with this: 'You pray to give your soul the words it wants to express. You pray because you believe. You pray because that's you—to pray is to tell God you believe and you hope. God doesn't listen with ears, you know. God is there, everywhere, I tell my grandchildren, and that means he hopes you're listening—to the people you love; and he hopes you're remembering him when you're listening, and when you're asking for something to happen in your prayers: you want him to be your witness, but remember, your life is your evidence!'

"I was up against the wall when she finished—I was reeling! I wrote down what she said [he did that often after leaving his patients, and sometimes their words got worked into his writing], and I read it to Flossie later. She said, 'Bill, you're always telling people how much you learn from your patients, from plain, ordinary, poor folks—so why the big surprise?' Still, there was a lot to think about—and I sure had her in mind (her and others like her) when I wrote that poem 'The Catholic Bells'!"

A great compliment was thus sent to that newly arrived American by her doctor—whose poem, actually, takes up lyrically what she was trying to get at in her own unself-conscious (but not analytic and not theological) manner: God as one to be called through our human devices of thought and sound. "Tho' I'm no Catholic . . ." Williams tells us right off. Then comes his deeply felt salute: "I listen hard when the bells / in the yellow-brick tower / of their new church / ring down the leaves . . ." In the lines that follow we meet some of his beloved Paterson patients—all of them ardent listeners to those bells, believers of what they are meant to indicate when they are heard: the importance of going to the building that houses them.

In a sense, I realized eventually, the bells, whose tolling authority and sanctity a poet chose to acknowledge and applaud, are very much a part of the mysteries that woman had conveyed to her visiting physician: God near us, with us, in ways that are indirect, suggestive rather than literal; for that's who we are, the ones who construct and figure meaning through hints and clues, through felt silences and touching sounds—recipients of all that happens around us, stirs us, gives us pause and thought, as the poet and physician William Carlos Williams knew on his own, but also gathered from others whom he got to help.

Private hurts trigger a public hurtfulness.

This year, as we were told in the news of killing rampages by suburban high schoolers, my mind returned to the young people, then (the 1960s) quaintly called "juvenile delinquents," who came to the child psychiatry clinic of the Children's Hospital in Boston, where I was working. In particular I remembered a boy I got to know when he was eleven and a girl who wasn't twelve when I first met her—both of them already in trouble with the law and already under careful scrutiny by school officials, who had turned to us doctors in alarm and perplexity, if not outright fear. Here is what I was told (and wrote down) about the boy: "He's a troublemaker and he's violent—he picks on kids younger than himself and beats them up badly. No one in the neighborhood where he lives likes him, and everyone is scared by his outbursts. He threatens people, and he follows through by hitting them, so that the police are called." I have left out identifying information—but there it was: a description of a child not yet an adolescent, seemingly headed for a long spell of prison.

As for the girl, she elicited from a woman who tried hard to "understand" her, a junior high school teacher, this gloomy comment: "She strikes out at any one who 'crosses' her—that's the word she uses. She'll say so-and-so 'crossed me and I won't let her get away with it.' I'll ask her what so-and-so did. She repeats herself: 'She crossed me.' If you press her for details, she comes up with nothing but threats: 'If she keeps it up, she'll pay for it.' She has actually threatened to 'beat up' those she considers her enemies. 'If I had a gun, I'd shoot you,' she told a girl her age in her class, who was minding her own business. When we asked her why she was threatening a classmate that way, she said that 'people defend their honor with a gun all over the world.' At that point we all knew [the school's teachers] that we had to go find help."

I was part of the "help" sought, and soon enough I was hearing the girl say what others claimed to have heard from her, even as I was reporting to a "supervisor." That experienced clinician, who also heard me out as I tried to figure what to make of the boy (and three others I was attempting to start "in treatment," two boys, one girl) stopped me in my tracks one day as I spoke of the two young individuals I'd known the longest, the boy who had been explicitly described as "violent" and the girl who made no bones about her desire to injure certain people with a gun, should she ever get one. Here is what I was, unforgettably, warned on paper (in a note) to keep in mind: "You'd best not forget that there is little prospect that you or I (or Sigmund Freud himself) can change and reverse the terrible chain of events that has culminated in this—in the two of them: children, they still are, who might live up to, deliver on, the menacing threats they've made. In our offices we can help undo the consequences of a punitively overbearing conscience; but to try to instill and nourish through conversations a conscience in a child who has none, who has never learned the importance of knowing the difference between right and wrong—that is another matter!"

A much practiced, savvy doctor was sending a message in such a way as to make his words memorable, and so they have been to me over the years—especially when I've been tempted to assume I can do successfully what I know well I won't be able to accomplish. Many times, alas, I've been asked to evaluate youths whose words and deeds have worried, mightily stunned, even terrified their dismayed, confused parents and teachers—all made needily hopeful for the capabilities a doctor is thought to bear (which promise a favorable outcome). But my medical teacher had warned me on another occasion that "often [no less!] there is little we can do clinically, however much we have learned, and so the best we can do is make quite clear what we can't do—and make quite clear how threatening a child or a teen-ager has turned out to be." He went further, told stories of children under ten who had used matches to set home fires that resulted in deaths, or of youngsters who had obtained guns, run amok, killed friends, relatives, neighbors, schoolmates—awful instances of murderousness in supposedly "innocent" children and youths.

Once vulnerable as babies, such boys and girls, a distinct but quite small minority (thank God) of their age-mates, have turned dangerous indeed. And some of us who have heard them out (or heard of them from others) can only shudder apprehensively—even as the rest of us, in the United States, have had recent cause to tremble at what the news tells us about the deeds of certain school children, whose personal suspicions and resentments, whose vengeful hates, have been permitted expression through acts enabled by available guns, wantonly used. "I have insisted in court sometimes," I was told by my supervising, elder physician, "that some children are a danger to themselves and to others, that they need to be locked up so they can't shoot and stab with impunity." Then, having stated the obvious (a doctor's melancholy everyday obligation), he mused more broadly, moving from psychology to sociology: "You do wonder why some of these very disturbed young people (with 'crazy ideas,' which a few of them will openly acknowledge) are able to get their hands on weapons that enable what is wild and weird in them to be visited upon others." So it sadly goes, he kept prompting me and others to consider—private hurts triggering a public hurtfulness.

Simone Weil tried to figure out morally who we humans are, what obligations we ought to feel and why, as we go about our permitted time on this planet.

S ome of us taking a course on contemporary religious thought in the middle of this century tried to understand the work of Simone Weil, reading her three books, *Waiting for God*, *The Need for Roots*, and *Gravity and Grace*—"one more difficult than the other," our professor playfully remarked. Yet he clearly wanted us to make the acquaintance of this almost legendary essayist, political philosopher, and member of the French resistance who stood up to Hitler's henchmen. We read with some difficulty the books urged on us. Nor did their author want us to have any easier time of it than she herself had had as she tried to figure out morally who we humans are, what obligations we ought to feel and why, as we go about our permitted time on this planet. Gradually we got to know this idiosyncratic, fussy, severely demanding writer—her exhortative and melancholy side, her bouts of skepticism that sooner or later yielded to a surprising, even startling insistence on the mind's necessary devotion to God.

In a way, she arraigned her own brilliance, declared its subjectivity before God, before the mysteries of worship and faith, as eminently desirable. She was well versed in Freud and Marx, but had her own manner of looking inward, or outward at the world and its workings. She was therefore a formidable antagonist to many who lived on the political left, who unreservedly embraced psychoanalysis (its secular interpretations of mental life) and Communism or socialism. This was their way of looking at money and power, a way she took seriously but wanted to forsake eventually in favor of the claims made for (and upon) us mortals by Jesus of Nazareth. His words and deeds, his fate in ancient Palestine she studied not only as a would-be believer, but as one who, in her own original-minded fashion, felt strongly that she, as an intellectual and as a political and social activist, had much to learn from the biblical narratives, pronouncements, and injunctions that make up the New Testament.

Two decades after I encountered Simone Weil in that college course, I resumed struggling to understand her ideas and ideals and tried to share what I'd learned about her through the effort of writing a biography. By then (the late 1970s) I was immersed in her articles and books, at times with admiration, at times with serious, even troubling reservations. It was then that I met her brother, Andre Weil, a most distinguished mathematician who taught at the Institute for Advanced Study at Princeton, and who had achieved his own breakthrough leadership as a rigorous thinker—a counterpart, in that regard, of his sister. I knew nothing of mathematics and had only heard of Andre Weil's various accomplishments as a theorist—the "Weil conjectures," no less. The phrase was an ironically fitting parallel to the suppositions and guesses of the ever-imaginative Simone.

To look at Andre Weil (I conjectured) was to get as close as it was possible to get to his sister both in appearance and manner. I recall noticing especially Andre Weil's eyes. They looked intently, took in the room where we sat, responded to questions put to him, then turned toward the distance a window offered, as if somewhere, beyond the then and there, answers awaited and were forthcoming to those who sought them.

I remember, too, some remarkable things he said, his eyes now back in the here and now of a conversation: "You have been studying my sister's work, so you must know that she defied the understanding of her life by others. She was sui generis, hard for people to know even when she was there among them. Who is she?—I was asked again and again. Once, when I told her what others wanted to know, she replied: 'It makes no difference—God matters, not the personality of this one or that one!' So I told one of the people later who was curious about her, that if she wanted to know who Simone is, she should try to think of her soul—its search for a home, for its Creator. You can imagine the look on the face that belonged to a member of the Parisian intelligentsia at the time! Through me, my sister Simone was once more walking her own road, speaking in words she knew well and liked to use, even if others, hearing them, scratched their heads in disbelief."

A pause then, followed by a wry smile, and this comment: "Of course, Simone had confronted her own disbelief in God, so she would naturally stir others to 'disbelief' when they heard of her or as I spoke of her! They respected her for her analytic thinking, but her thinking had taken her far from university seminar rooms. She no longer held her head high with ideas that held others spellbound; she was herself spellbound. She was on her knees in [Catholic] churches, praying and praying to God." More memories followed, as Andre Weil "spoke of" his sister.

When I learned that he died, at ninety-two, in early August 1998, I heard and saw him in my head: the elusive and brilliant brother who kept bringing us closer, as he summoned words, to the heart, the rock-bottom spirit of his difficult-to-grasp yet powerfully pressing sister—both of them towering giants of reflection, gifts to the rest of us to keep considering hard and long.

*"Do you really think the pope prayed for those three
mass murderers, Hitler, Stalin, Mussolini?" I asked
Dorothy Day.*

In recent months, while a war-time pontiff's attitudes toward mid-cen-
tury European totalitarianism became a subject of written discussion
(as in *Hitler's Pope* and the response to it by reviewers and other readers), I have often remembered conversations on that issue with Dorothy
Day, whom I was privileged to know. In particular I heard Dorothy Day
talk at great length about Pius XII and, of course, John XXIII, whom (un-
surprisingly) she much revered. She found her very own way of connecting
with Pope Pius, who (so she once put it) "had to wake up every morning
at the Vatican and pray for that terrible trio of dictators during the 1930s
and 1940s." I recall being stunned by that comment, and told her why (I
was tape-recording our talks then, at work on a biography of her). "Do
you really think the pope prayed for those three mass murderers, Hitler,
Stalin, Mussolini?" I asked. A few seconds of thought, followed by a firm
nod, and then this: "Oh, he must have prayed and prayed for them. You
pray for the devil, and those three were agents of the devil!"

Yes, I understood her line of theological reasoning. I could see that she
wasn't being provocative or in any way inclined to overlook the murderous

horror that descended on Europe in the name of Nazism or fascism or, too, the Stalinism that had killed decisively the so-called socialism Lenin and his cohorts had claimed to offer Russia and the world. Still, I was confused, maybe incredulous—maybe, even, more alarmed and irritated than I knew myself to be. Her eyes had taken measure of my stilled voice, my impassive face, and so this comment: "I have gotten into a lot of trouble saying what I just did to my old friends. They hated Hitler and Stalin, and so did I—for all they did, all they stood for. But you see, we here [at the Catholic Worker hospitality house where we then sat] will be found praying for people on death row, on their way to the noose or the electric chair—not because we are at all on their side, as their supporters or friends, but because they weren't born to do the evil they did, weren't sent here by the Lord to do that. A moment ago we got close to what I mean to tell you, what I believe—that even the monsters Hitler or Stalin are fallen sinners, and we cry and pray for them, for all of us who can stumble, do stumble."

I followed her, but I was unsatisfied. My mind visited concentration camps by way of pictures I'd seen and through the words I'd heard from a dear Jewish friend who had miraculously survived one of them. A nearby cup of coffee to her lips, a glance toward her books, all those novels of Dostoevski and Dickens that she so much treasured, and then a further explanation: "My friends tell me that it was wrong for the pope to sign up with Mussolini and Hitler—those pacts he made with them, the diplomatic agreements. They were a 'scandal' [she had been told]—and I see the point, though I remind myself of what Stalin said, that famous question: 'How many tanks does the Vatican have?' There was a cold-blooded murderer [Stalin] who knew the basic tactics of power, and Hitler was another one. I ask myself what the pope should have done or could have done. He had no tanks to stop Hitler or Stalin, as they both knew. Who am I to say what was right for the pope to do? Oh, I suppose I am Catholic, a believer, and it's up to me to pray for the pope, that he do what's right to do."

There was much discussion of that last matter: what ought to have been done by the Vatican's leader decades earlier in this century. I dare tell her that I never could have prayed for Hitler's soul, were I old enough to do so when she was alive, as she said she had done. And pressed by her, I tell her I'd have prayed that he would get killed. Her look of disapproval in response prompts me to change the subject. Finally, I ask her directly whether she had ever imagined a course of action by Pius XII different from the one he took. She muses for seconds, shakes her head, then her face becomes animated: "Oh, I had some thoughts, yes (you folks [psychiatrists] call them 'fantasies'); I remember sitting in church and wishing (I wasn't praying, just wishing) that the pope had thrown all caution to the winds, asked to go to a concentration camp and stay there, or that he had faced down the Nazis, the S.S., told them they could arrest him, jail him, shoot him dead with their guns, because he wasn't going to surrender to their evil. He'd scream his defiance of it, die, if need to be, resisting it. But then I heard my mother's voice saying, as she always did, 'Come now, Dorothy; be practical.' Later, out of church, I had this realization come to me: The pope is not Jesus; the pope is not a martyr to truth and justice, to the good, as Jesus was. The pope is an officer in an organization—that's his tragedy, our tragedy, Christ's. We fail the Lord all the time—popes do, and cardinals do, and we parishioners do. That is as far as my mind could take me then—or now, I'm afraid."

In a moment she had to leave to help make coffee and soup for the many "guests," the poor, the ailing, the down-and-out ones, whom she gladly and constantly served—maybe her way of seeking salvation, and maybe her way, finally, of addressing popes and cardinals, never mind the high-and-mighty government officials with whom they, the august leaders of the Catholic church, deign to meet, bargain, and deal.

Afterword

When I was a college student, I had the good fortune to be taught by a teacher, Perry Miller, who kept insisting that we in the classroom "venture forth—out of these fancy dorms and libraries," he put it; and then a memorable pause: "into the world where people learn from one another, courtesy of serendipity." How perplexed we listeners became in response to that remark! Why such a departure, when this was the very place where we were supposed to be doing a considerable amount of learning from others, known as first-rate teachers? Next, the words spoken, a hand picked up chalk and our eyes were summoned to a written gesture, our ears given a break: the word "serendipity" was there for us to witness, ponder. I can still recall the first sound I heard, after the stillness of a bunch of us dominated the room: "a college board word," said my sitting neighbor, his face's evident savvy no match for the scorn his whisper managed to convey—and a second later, this cynical follow-up: "You get into this place if you can throw words like that at others."

Silence on my part and on the part of my neighbor, and college friend—and on with the lecture. But after we had left that lecture hall, the word "serendipity" kept asserting itself in my mind—I didn't really know what it meant; so, back in my dorm room I turned to the dictionary, got my answer.

Weeks later, during a so-called tutorial I was lucky to take with Professor Miller, the word "serendipity" returned for my ears' attention: "We can learn a lot through what might be called the 'grace of serendipity.'" Silence, as I wondered at the threesome just tossed my way. Then an observant teacher's apology, amplification: "Sorry to toss that comment your way. I was just trying to break myself out of all the expected ways of thinking a classroom can push on us, and say through the use of a word that we can learn a hell of a lot in this life every day, outside classrooms and libraries, by letting our everyday life be our teacher: the serendipitous is luck, good or bad, coming our way, and that luck can teach us a lot, if we're ready to say 'yes, sure enough, what's happened can be a big teaching, learning moment in my life.'" More words, as a teacher spotted a student's evident perplexity. Then came interpretative help—the essence of which I finally could comprehend, and to this day and time find important to keep in mind: lots of learning can come our way, suddenly, unexpectedly, surprisingly, accidentally—and yet soon enough become an important part of our personal lives, affecting how and what we think, believe, and say.

As I look back at the essays this book provides, I keep returning to that time with a college teacher, because his comment on life's flow, including its serendipitous moments, helped me understand much of what I was so constantly regarding, trying to say, affirming, figuring out, explaining to myself and others—what still figures in me, his one-time student, then his student, still, who wrote essays in response to what befell a life's moments, its way. Again and again, in these essays, I remark upon incidents, encounters, impasses, and resolutions thereof—a wayfarer, as are we all, trying to get through time, events, and responsively wondering about them, their meaning to him, or with respect to life's overall significance. In a sense, then, these are essays that tell of a person's journey through time, space, and place (now straightforward, now aimless, sometimes even perplexing).

Once the poet and physician Dr. William Carlos Williams became, for a moment, a briefly forceful teacher of mine: "When we write a personal essay," he remarked in his usual insistent way, "we're often writing so that we can figure out what matters, and why, what happened, and why, or what to do—and so with written words, we're sharing our experiences, our great hopes, our disappointments, our ups and downs: all of that, our mind's effort to share what we went through with others, and maybe, in so doing, join our self, the scribbler, to others, the fellow travelers who accompany us as we try to figure out what happened and why." With those words of a great teacher I was so lucky to know came an explanation, in a sense, of my life, its work done in so many places; and with those words I can conclude my latter-day remarks about long-ago written words, and bid a big thank-you to this book's kind and thoughtful editor, and to its present-day readers, my unknown and accidental friends.

Acknowledgments

Special thanks to Peter Berg, Head of Special Collections, Michigan State University Libraries, and archivist Anne-Marie Rachman for their assistance in putting together this edition and their continuing stewardship of the Robert Coles Papers and the *DoubleTake* Archive. The editor gratefully acknowledges the continuing support of David Gift, Vice Provost of Libraries, Computing, and Technology, and Clifford Haka, Director of Libraries, Michigan State University. Patrick Kindig, an Honors College undergraduate research assistant, worked diligently and ably on several research and editorial tasks related to the production of this book.

These columns were originally published in *America*. They are reprinted with the permission of Robert Coles and America Press, Inc., 106 West 56th Street, New York, NY 10019.

ROBERT COLES is a child psychiatrist and professor emeritus of psychiatry and medical humanities at Harvard University where he was named James Agee Professor of Social Ethics in the Graduate School of Education. Coles is a Pulitzer Prize–winning author, a MacArthur Foundation Fellow, and a recipient of the National Endowment for the Humanities' National Humanities Medal and the prestigious Presidential Medal of Freedom, the nation's highest civilian honor. He has had more than sixty honorary degrees conferred upon him. He is the author of more than ninety books. Coles is best known for his books that explore children's moral, political, and spiritual sensibilities. He is also known as an eloquent spokesman for community service, civil rights, and the public responsibilities of academics, writers, and intellectuals—subjects of books like *The Call of Stories*, *A Call to Service*, *The Secular Mind*, *Lives of Moral Leadership*, *Bruce Springsteen's America*, and, most recently, *Lives We Carry with Us: Profiles of Moral Courage*, edited by David D. Cooper. Coles has written literary criticism, numerous biographies, reviews, poetry, social commentary, several children's books, and regular columns for the *New Republic*, *New Yorker*, *New Oxford Review*, *America*, and *American Poetry Review*. In addition, Coles is founder and editor of the award-winning documentary magazine *DoubleTake* and the author of numerous works of documentary nonfiction, including *The Story of Ruby Bridges*, *The Old Ones of New Mexico*, and *Doing Documentary Work*.

First appointed as a Teaching Fellow in Psychiatry at the Harvard Medical School in 1955, Coles's career at Harvard University—chronicled recently in *Handing One Another Along*—spans forty-seven years of teaching, writing, and service to communities of hard-pressed people, especially children, from Alaska to the favelas of Rio de Janeiro. Coles is a pragmatic moralist whose books and life are witness to the reality of the moral life at work in the world. Numerous critical studies stress Coles's representative status as a thinker, writer, teacher, and activist in the American grain.

⌣

DAVID D. COOPER is professor of Writing, Rhetoric, and American Cultures at Michigan State University and former Senior Editor of *Fourth Genre: Explorations in Nonfiction* (MSU Press). Cooper edited Coles's *Lives We Carry with Us: Profiles of Moral Courage* (2010), and he has published several articles and essays on Robert Coles, including "Doing and Learning with Robert Coles" (1994) and "Moral Literacy" (1996). He was a regular contributor to *DoubleTake*, an award winning documentary magazine founded and edited by Robert Coles.

⌣